Thomas Tapper

The Music Life and How to Succeed in It

Thomas Tapper

The Music Life and How to Succeed in It

ISBN/EAN: 9783337084714

Printed in Europe, USA, Canada, Australia, Japan

Cover: Foto ©Thomas Meinert / pixelio.de

More available books at **www.hansebooks.com**

THE

MUSIC LIFE

AND

HOW TO SUCCEED IN IT.

BY

THOMAS TAPPER.

Art is the child of Nature ; yes,
Her darling child, in whom we trace
The features of the mother's face,
Her aspect and her attitude,
All her majestic loveliness
Chastened and softened and subdued
Into a more attractive grace,
And with a human sense imbued.—KERAMOS.

PHILADELPHIA:

THEODORE PRESSER

1892.

WM. F. FELL, & CO.,
ELECTROTYPERS AND PRINTERS,
1220-24 SANSOM STREET, PHILADELPHIA.

TO

JOHN WILLIS CONANT,

IN FRIENDLY

REMEMBRANCE.

———

> I bless the time
> When my good falcon made her flight across
> Thy father's ground.
> —*The Winter's Tale.*

PREFACE.

If it is necessary to apologize for the appearance of this volume of Talks about the phases of the Music Life it may be said that no stimulus can be too strong which aims to show the young American musician the serious nature of his task. That the musical profession is more or less characterized by a host of art-mongers needs no proof from me. To offset their unhealthy practices is the duty of the rest. I think it may be said that earnestness in the art-world is a sure forerunner of success, provided one can direct it forcibly under the guidance of educated ability. All these factors are necessary,

Education in Music is not to be had by spending a life-time in looking at it through a microscope. One must get out of it and into other things, now and again, for pleasure, health, and hints. I have spoken freely of the arts in general and of other lines of intellectual inquiry not strictly artistic, not unknowingly; it is because all these subjects are full to overflowing with suggestions for the musician that I bring them prominently forward. And further, I have suggested to my audience many side-studies, not because I think every one will or should undertake them all, but because each may find among them some one or two to his taste.

Such Talks as these should take place, in substance, between every teacher and his students. They bring their own good.

Boston, 15th of April, 1891.

CONTENTS.

---

vii

PART IV.

SOME SPECIAL THEMES.

CHAPTER.   PAGE

PART V.

HELPS.

PART VI.

SITUATION.

PART VII.

A BUNCH OF LETTERS.

PART VIII.

THE LAST TALKS.

x

THE MUSIC LIFE

AND

HOW TO SUCCEED IN IT.

PART I.—THE MISSION OF MUSIC.

CHAPTER I.

THE FIRST TALK.

I'll give you a verse to this note, that I made yesterday in despite of my Invention.—*As You Like It* (Act II, Scene V).

Great good comes from companionship when it is of the best.   We talk to a friend in direct and simple language; that is well, plain talk is best for many reasons.   There is mental and physical economy in it, there is life in it, and, when it springs spontaneously from the heart, you may believe there is sincerity in it.   Thus the short words of a language are our home words; listen to the conversation about your fire-side and you will learn that this is true.   Of them the pronouns are very strong, and you may note that in every language they are short,

9

generally of one syllable and of few letters. They mean much when they are directed, for they are binding words; mankind will forever feel their influence. We will speak, then, familiarly, in this and all the following talks, because in this way we can talk better and because it is more companionable, for, as I said in the first words of this paragraph—great good comes from companionship when it is the best, and that is what we offer one another.

We are to talk of art; not so much, this time, of beginnings as of those phases and developments which we are forever encountering but which we seldom consider. We shall take for our themes some of the many matters that constantly come before us, delicately hinting that we pay heed to them, but to which we do not, in truth, pay so much heed after all. As to their importance in the daily life of an artist I will ask you to reserve your opinion until these talks are done ; they are the last, perhaps, we shall ever have, and this thought leads me to say, not, indeed all there is to be said, for I could not do that, but to say what I can in the best and clearest way to you. I promise you that there shall be in every one of these talks a leading thought,—the mid-rib of the leaf—, and it shall be my endeavor so to present this thought that any one who follows it shall find therein practical, serviceable good—, I shall try to show you the veining of the leaf as well as its mid-rib.

There are some thoughts that I shall repeat many times, as we go on, I do so purposely; a nail is seldom driven its full length at a single blow. I shall, too, point out how you may be constantly increasing your employment. I do this also intentionally for I would not have you find too soon in life a place so comfortable, so nicely yielding to all the desires and weaknesses of your nature that you may never discover it to be of any use to exert yourself. Believe me when I say the more you strive the more you become; the self is always with you and the more and better that self is the greater is the gain to you, for you cannot leave it. Youth-struggle seems to be the pillow for age-rest. Thought well invested pays large returns; you cannot learn to manage this kind of investment with too much care. Hence the constant incentive I keep before you, to work, is well-meant. One needs but a very little practical experience in art to learn that not until it is established upon a foundation of practicability and meaning can one follow it to advantage. Artists neither dwell in fairy-glens nor live on sun-beams. This picture is usually the fond desire of those who never exert themselves to dispel the illusion. But it is true that art is uplifting. It enables a rare intelligence to illumine life with bright pictures *founded on something.*

I am constantly surprised as I study the motive with which many enter the music life expecting to win success in it. I ask myself why they do not meet the question of their own intention face to face, why they will not choose an objective point, find out how to reach it, what will be the cost in personal endeavor, the value of what they desire as a power to be exercised in society, the need of it, its power to develop the nobler self within, its place and value in a serious life. But one is greatly astonished to learn that a great many will not think of these things; not only this, but they never conceive art to assume such connections. To be an artist one must live the life of an artist; the semblance of it will not do. The thoughts and hopes, fears and aspirations of an artist must enter into it, to give form and color, strength and tendency. You must put heart in what you do; your work must have depth. We all reverence toil but toil alone is not enough; it must have soul. "You think you can get every thing by grinding—music, literature, and painting. You will find it grievously not so; you can get nothing but dust by mere grinding. Even to have the barley-meal out of it, you must have the barley first; and that comes by growth, not grinding." * In one form carbon is but a bit of coal, in another intensity it is a diamond.

---

* John Ruskin.

CHAPTER II.

MUSIC AS AN ART.

The entire vitality of art depends upon its being either full of truth, or full of use.—JOHN RUSKIN.

Music appeals to us in a two-fold relation, for itself alone as an art, for the practice we put it to as a business. As the music-art creates a world of thought within, so it builds up a world of business relations without; and while it gives form and expression to the inner life it, at the same time, is the means of our bread winning. At the very outset of his career the young artist is obliged to consider this two-fold relation of the music-art and, though he may be unaware of it, he is strongly influenced by the one relation at the expense of the other; this inclination characterizes the young musician and unconsciously he forms habits of thought and activity that will remain with him for life. According as he inclines to one or the other of these two phases of the music-life in early years, so the worth of all after activity will be.

From the very beginning of practice in music there is a contention between these two main phases that is most difficult to consider. The young musician is in doubt as to how much time and attention to give to art when his time and knowledge have a certain fixed worth. The temptation to sacrifice all available study time to money earning is, in the majority of cases, so very strong that fair consideration of both these phases is never given. A career is begun in prosperity and because it is improperly followed and because, by coming to an educational standstill the musician fails to keep up with all that is latest and best in his art-specialty, it gradually loses value; the inactive teacher falls behind, commands an ever decreasing public and has the pain of seeing himself quietly but surely forgotten in the musical art and business of his time. Hence it is my earnest advice to you that in the very beginning of your music-life you give consideration to these questions, then you may undertake the practice of your profession understandingly, you will know how much money you need to earn and how much time you may call your own, and believe me, there will come a day when you will think your richest possession is the hours that you may be free to command; there is a far greater fund of power, pleasure and real life in them than in all the money you can earn. Thus Time and Money are the representative powers of the two phases of the music-life which we are to consider here, namely, the Art and the Business; both deserve our closest attention. Let us see what it will reveal.

As to the motive that leads you into the art-life I will not inquire, but let me say that I address only those of you who practice art for its own sake, who feel that the richest reward for activity is not money alone but the satisfaction of having stamped your name and character on a piece of work of which you may say—I am not ashamed of it. "If you adopt an art to be your trade," says Robert Louis Stevenson, "weed your mind at the outset of all desire for money. What you may decently expect, if you have some talent and much industry, is such an income as a clerk will earn with a tenth, or perhaps a twentieth of your nervous output. Nor have you the right to look for more; in the wages of the life, not in the wages of the trade, lies your reward; the work is here the wages." You must love your labor; unless you do there will never enter into your art-life that sweet sunshine of pardonable pride which comes from the remembrance of tasks well done and life well lived. A mark that you love art and deserve its rewards is shown in laborious zeal that expends itself as long and willingly upon the detail as upon the whole of a great work. You must learn to be candid with yourself; never ashamed to acknowledge the frequent fault; proud if you may set it aright; as wise and just, as far seeing and careful in your kingdom as if you ruled a broad land. If you feel within yourself the power to move onward, the unquenchable impulse to press to the front, if discouragement does not seize you for its own, if repeated failure only makes you stronger, then surely you are God-blessed and the art of tone which you so love may be proud of you.

The demands upon an artist, both from within and without, render the art-life in nearly all its particulars most unique, well nigh inexplicable to one who is not in touch with its moods and phases. That we sometimes regard art as a goddess whose followers lead a Bohemian existence is a fault of our making. There is not one phase of art-life that will not admit the closest scrutiny, that may not stand on common-sense principles as firmly as upon that æsthetic foundation we are so prone to provide for it. One must admit that the business-principle may not apply everywhere in art; it is too weak, for example, to grapple with that uncertain power—inspiration; nevertheless, the business-principle may be applied to such a number of art-phases that one becomes better acquainted with those regions where it is powerless to go, in the very care he takes to trace it where it may apply. The fountain of art we may examine at our leisure, and learn much about it, but of the hidden spring which provides the spray that flashes like a shower of diamonds in the sunshine we can know nothing, for it takes its being in the hand of God and returns thither.

At the very outset in the Music Life let us inquire what are the duties that devolve upon us when longing, thought and opportunity so constellate that we may determine to lead the art-life. This duty, we see at once, is three-fold, duty to God, duty to Man, duty to Art, and I have named them in their order. How the incidents and circumstances of life in all its relationships combine to make us uncertain as to what we should do! No one who has followed a serious line of thought for a few years can have failed to learn this. Yet as the impurity in water will settle in time so we come to a clearer understanding of our own intimate connections. We learn that we are not our own creators, that we have fellow-men, that whatever life-work we adopt develops us, makes us what we are in giving us a chance to erect a worthy monument by our own endeavor. Let me tell you now that it is not this or that profession that gives you worth and importance, it is what you do in it. It may be great work or little that you do, what we want to know is how you do it. In respect of intellectual worth we are like nations. Greece is very small in square miles but wonderful in the

2

history of its doings. So, too, England is of little extent, less than many of our States, but it is an *intense* land. It "stretches by an illusion to the dimensions of an empire. The innumerable details, the crowded succession of towns, cities, cathedrals, castles, and great and decorated estates, the number and power of the trades and guilds, the military strength and splendor, the multitude of rich and remarkable people, the servants and equipages,— all these catching the eye, and never allowing it to pause, hide all boundaries, by the impression of magnificence and endless wealth."* The dignity of your office reflects discredit upon you if you are insincere in what you allow it to draw from you. Wisdom looks not to your fame but to your aim. It credits accordingly.

One is constantly surprised to note how very little attention is given to art as a means for moral development. Nothing in the world of work can do more for the moral man than study in the arts and sciences; and you should feel proud when I say to you that there is no field of labor at your command capable of yielding more to you as a child of God and a brother among men than the very art-life you have chosen for your life-companion. Look for the truth of this and you will

---

* R. W. Emerson (English Traits).

acknowledge it to be so, and accept it also as a truth that where art has produced a failure anything else would have done the same; for the seed of failure slumbers in the man, not in the noble themes for thought that surround him.

Besides the gains of music-life you must come to the consideration of art in daily life. At first it is difficult to bring about sympathetic union between the surroundings of a commonplace existence and those lofty idealities of art that are so apt to illumine the future of the musician. This question, like that relating to personal bearing in the home, is only to be decided by each one for the self; it will be found that art as we must practice it is the result of certain concessions which our circumstances demand us to make to our chosen activity, while it is none the less the peculiar adaptation we make of such advantages as have come to us. It will exist anywhere provided there is a nourishing mental atmosphere. Learning is prone to take up its abode in *outre* places; genius lurks in many an out-of-the-way spot. One thinks of this, wandering along the Bonny Doon; and one also thinks that any rich gift of nature regarded with common sense may be made comfortable. A wonderful power of art is that it so strongly influences us, that for its sake we better our surroundings, we constantly strive to entertain our goddess in a finer mansion. Familiarity with art topics makes us love the beautiful; having learned this, we next begin to look for beauty in this place and that; then we look for it everywhere, and to our growing wonder—we find it. It is true that the deeper interest we take in art the more we strive to make all about us worthy of what we would have present. To the true lover of the beautiful who is an earnest student there is no question that so quickly resolves itself as this of art in daily life.

It would seem that we need a new turn of phrase as a logical offset to that common expression "art-lover", something of the sense of "art-understand-er"; and I would distinguish between them in this manner: The "art-lover" is one upon whose finer emotions the beautiful acts; "art-understanders" are those upon whose reason and judgment the beautiful acts, touching the emotions on the way thither; for not until the effect of beauty acting upon us has filtrated through the emotions and the cause thereof been carefully examined by the judgment, is appreciation keen or opinion of value. Now we know that there are art-lives made up entirely of the super-excitation to which our emotional faculties are subject; and ninety-nine per cent. of the vagaries of thought, expression, and action commonly attributed to the art-life in general is to be traced to those beings who . have been gifted with more ability than judgment—or, to say the same thing in plainer words, with more ability to do than common-sense to know how to do. Genius is not alone the ability to perform, but the cool, discriminating judgment that sees how to do, in the most logical and finished manner. There is nothing in art contrary to the principles of truth, worth, manliness and common-sense. Instances apparently to the contrary are the best arguments in support of this statement. The common opinion among writers and artists of all schools is that no one can win true success who depends solely on natural gifts, but all are of one voice in saying that earnest hard work and plenty of it, diligence, perseverance, frugal hope, are the only factors that can successfully develop natural ability. Of course I take it that you understand this one thing about the genius—that he is a wonder because nature does not fashion him commonly and that he combines all the qualities of natural ability and hard work to a transcendent degree. The majority of art-workers are not of his class. I do not consider you all, individually, to be rich in the pure ore of genius to a degree of value beyond compare, but rather as well-loaded veins which, at the very outset, show what they possess and exhibit an evenness in the production that gives one faith in the worth.

At the outset of the music-life you will be called upon to decide in how far the art you practice must yield to the business you make of it.   How much art do you strive for and how much money? You must at once condescend to consider your knowledge for its market value; what do you offer to the public and what do you require in return for it? If you are in expectation of your living from the people, if you look to them for your support, they have a right to know the value of what you hold to be your stock in trade.   This is a true relation too little considered.   There is no greater field for imposition than in art-teaching; no relationship between person and public that should receive fairer, more honest consideration on the part of the one appealing to the public than that of the artist.   I think many enter the art-life with an exaggerated idea of what are the gains that come therefrom.   Many attempt to find the mine of art-riches, and see that years of labor and expensive study are necessary before even the probability of just remuneration may be entertained; at this discovery a few are honest enough to withdraw, but a great many stop short and become permanently engaged in that of which they know little, which is not, however one regards it, an honest business principle.   And assuredly the first duty of a person who announces himself a lover of the true and beautiful in art is honesty in transaction. It may be safely said that the true artists are those who begin study with no thought of immediate gain and with but little expectation of great gain at any time. The would-be artist who enters the field primarily for money may get it and he may not. As a paying investment in which one puts little and expects much, art is not to be recommended. Ruskin, addressing himself to young architects, has said: "You may like making money exceedingly; but if it come to a fair question, whether you are to make £500 less by this business or spoil your building, and you choose to spoil your building, there's an end of you." *

Judging between these two representatives of our music students the willing worker has much to hope for, many glorious models to copy, and no end of satisfaction in the very labor that comes to his hands. The money-seeker, on the contrary, cannot look about him and find very many instances of what one may style the financial success in art, and he may carry his investigations into the field of literature and the result will be the same. One finds innumerable aspirants, a few successful, or said to be, and the majority gaining neither fame nor a living. These are hard words to write,

---

* See his lecture on " Influence of Imagination in Architecture.''

but, nevertheless, they ought to be printed everywhere in letters of gold; art-life does not pay;
neither does professional life, and both demand
more severe and long sustained labor than any line
of activity one can undertake; not only this, but
they demand a long, unpaid apprenticeship that
may or may not turn out successfully; if it does
the salary earned during the first years is not great,
while the labor that wins it is.   I hope no one will
charge me with lack of reverence for art when I
thus subject it to the close scrutiny of the business
man.   Whoever enters art to make a living from
it will suffer very material thoughts to act upon
his surroundings if he sees want and necessity
near at hand.   To-day the money question in art
is unavoidable to all but one in a thousand.   All
works of art come before the people through the
channels of trade.   There is need of money to pay
fine artists for coming before the public; money
needed to hold together large musical organiza-
tions; money to requite the critic for his labor;
money demanded from the public in return for the
intellectual pleasure of hearing musical works
performed; money required between teacher and
student, the primary step of all, and when we
come to this we are arrived at a point that directly
interests you as a young teacher.   We ask what
you offer the public, what you consider is its

worth, how you intend to dispose of it, what is the value of your time and how much of it you are willing to surrender for an equivalent in money.

Before considering these matters closely let me repeat that of all your possessions none are so valuable to you in the first years of the teaching-life, as time. Therewith you gain the opportunity to carry on study in circumstances of a value that has never before been yours; you are working with a few students of your own; in every one of them there is a wonderful amount of suggestion; an unexplored world lies before you, and the time to study any such phase of life is when you have the time, and if you ever shall have the time it will be in the first years of your teaching when you are striving to work your way into the professional world. When you first begin to teach determine just how much money you think will *suffice* you for the coming year, determine how much time it will require to earn it, then you may form somewhat of an idea concerning what time remains to you for your own work. It is no part of the divine conception that men should spend all their forces in seeing *how much* money they can accumulate in a given time. That you are not pressed with a paying business at once is no reason you should spend your time in idleness, waiting for business to knock at your door; you will find that you must devote time and close attention toward directing business your way, then trusting that it will be pleased to walk in and take up quarters with you. When I look upon the first years of the artist's after-school life I see no idleness in it.

CHAPTER III.

MUSIC AS A BUSINESS.

" Nothing hurts worse than frivolity; nothing unfits for business more, or forms worse habits for success, or wastes the time in which we might mould the future, and nothing leaves less return."—CUNNINGHAM GEIKIE.

An art and the business of it combine to make a profession. The dignity of a profession is in the hands of those who practice it. In this short talk I purpose bringing before you those small matters of business which, though apparently trifling, are a solid basis in themselves. Considering an instructor's knowledge as the merchandise of his business we notice at once that it differs in one very important particular from material stock in trade, and that is this: one can dispose of the same general fund time and time again and still possess it; one does not need constantly to replenish. But one is not to conclude therefrom that to have obtained a certain limited amount of art education is enough. Those who do this, quickly come to a standstill, then they begin gradually to go backwards. You must move onward in art as in aught else; you must gain from year to year, so that your worth as a professional and as a man may be constantly greater. If, as you grow older, you fail to gather knowledge, experience, fortune, and ability, you will certainly lose the first worth of your education judged in its value to others; for in education as in other lines of work the best is most in demand and is the better paid for.

At the very beginning of your career you may accept it as an unvarying truth that what is known as a smattering has no real worth. The best of the world of to-day is too busy to give any heed to the inactive or to the charlatan. You will find the possession of an education to be a great care; while it is in itself a talent that you must increase, it must at the same time be watched and adapted to widely different needs. No material possession can require of you greater care than does education. They who give little thought or application to what they know do not possess knowledge, but a shadow of it. Though education is indestructible it can, nevertheless, secrete itself so deeply that we cannot reach it, cannot make it available at any instant. Education that is so withdrawn from momentary use is of little value to a learner. Hence one of the first business duties of an artist is ever to have the intellectual and technical possession in the best possible condition. This is simply to fulfil a business relation.

If, as an instructor in any branch of art, you appeal to the public for your living, and that is what we all do in one way or another, you are in duty bound to have sufficient regard for health that you may be physically able to fulfil your promises.   If you contract with the public or with the directors of an institution to teach six hours per day, you owe it to them and to yourself to take all the care in your power to be physically capable of fulfilling that agreement.   Any lack of care on your part, in this regard, is the violation of a business relation and is not right.   Punctuality is a business law that you will be called upon to observe, and it will be your duty to teach others to observe it; you can give your students no better example than that of punctuality.   They must learn it, and no one can better teach them than you.   Punctuality finds its application in every contract you make; in every debt you assume; in every relationship you form.   The business man's punctuality in the one matter of correspondence is of immense value to him, and his observance of it here will tend to make him observe it elsewhere; as a result he will become, in this one respect at least, a better man. The debt punctually paid, the contract fulfilled to the day and to the minutest item, the letter answered at once, all these things combine to give the business man his standing, and that is something he guards jealously. You will find many things in the business man's thrift and tact well worth accepting for practice in art, which some think too beautiful to be judged after the manner of more common things.

It is not business-like for you to agree to perform what you cannot; one or two bits of experience in this particular will be of more value to you than all one could possibly write. There is no harm, however, in one advising you to have faith in your ability, and to examine all conditions before agreeing to them. A little thought spent in tracing out relationships will give you an exact idea of your duty to self, to student and to public. As you value your own business hours, pay respect to the time of others, and do not consume it unnecessarily. As it is a moral sin for you to waste your own time it is even a greater one for you to be the cause of a loss of time to others, for thereby you take what is not in your power nor that of any other man to give. Time and training are the two factors of importance in every line of activity.

If in art practice you have more regard for the money gain than for the value you surrender you pay no heed to the first and foremost of business relations—namely, justness of values, worth of thing given for thing received. In education this simple principle has far wider application than in the exchange of materials, because the instructor forms in his student the future man or woman, gives the bent of character, tendency, habit and way of thought.   If all those relationships are forgotten whereby the personality in the instructor is lost to sight in its action upon the personality of the student, and thought be given to gain in money alone, the instructor has defrauded the student out of an opportunity to obtain an amount of manliness and precise training.   The money consideration is frequently necessary and just between any two people, it need not affect the value of the staple of the transaction, but there are times when it is the last thing in importance.   Money cannot pay a teacher who teaches from the heart nor can money alone give the instructor the inspiration necessary to do his best for the student.   As it is the union of the very qualities in an instructor not appealed to by money that does most for the learner, it is evident that it is not a business principle in art to labor with no other thought than for financial gain.

The question of Popularity will sometimes come before you.   A little thought,—it does not require much,—will make it clear that you cannot afford to be popular.   The price is a surrender of too much that is necessary *to your gradual growth*.   To fulfil the capricious demands of the moment you must lose sight of your future, and that you cannot afford. There is a difference between popularity and an acknowledgment from the public of lasting value ; the one is a loud cry made strong because this man raises his voice at the sound of his neighbor's ; by and by he thinks better of it and holds his peace. An acknowledgment of lasting value is the decree of the thinkers of the day, of the intelligent ones, to whom others look for direction. Remember that popularity is an expensive possession and is no safe indication of merit or worth.

Your attitude to the public is a business relation of much importance. Think how the people about you make their estimate of your worth. This will show you that there are many relationships of your making about which you may think little but to which others attach much importance. Any one who regards you has a right to conclude, if your personal relations are not of the best, that your low associations and high ideals are not to be reconciled. The way you manage your affairs out of art is a safe indication as to how you will conduct them in it. If your business principles are slack it counts very strongly against you ; if prompt and accurate these . two qualities are put to your credit. Perhaps of all your friends not more than two or three look closely, interestedly at your ways of life, but these are the two or three whose opinion is of untold value to you.   If you win any honor it is these who study how you bear it; they notice if you are led easily into this thing and that, if you are careful to become not merely an artist but a true man or woman; they study the thrift of your business management and how you place yourself and your business before the public.   If you assume unnecessary importance every one smiles, as much in pity as in mirth, at your self-exaggeration.   If you continually change your business methods, faith in you is lost; you must establish a line of activity and stick to it before you can win the trust and good will of others.   A certain young painter thinks it is worth something to him to have the society papers say that he resembles Vandyck "about the eyes." Perhaps he does not think that he would, more to the credit of himself and his art, actually resemble Vandyck *about the brush*.   Another who would come before the public announces that his work has been highly commended by this one and that; forgetting that the thinking person knows very well that " this one and that " can form no just estimate whatever of such work.   Another, a pianist, announces a *répertoire* of solo numbers " including works of all composers," thus making it appear that his knowledge of the best works is unusually extensive when, in reality, he knows no others than the few of each writer that are fitted to his technic, thus giving evidence that there is a kind of half honesty which is the most downright dishonesty. These instances may appear to be little matters, but according as one regards them they make or unmake the man and woman.

It is not uncommon to hear that the musician and artist are not good business managers. Any one who will closely scrutinize the art-life in its varying phases will find that, like all other activities, it creates its own particular expenses, that the more extensive is the business and social relation, the more forms of outlay are necessary; but one cannot find any reason why the artist should not have a just regard for values, why he should be a careless spender instead of a thrifty manager. It is true that art appeals to the emotions, *but to the emotions through the judgment.* Philanthropy does as much. Every artist and art-teacher can apply the same economic principles to his earning as the most careful artisan. He can be frugal, can plan to save money, can establish his business, whether it be little or much, on as secure a basis as any other worker. He can contribute more than a great many to the building of the nation. There are numberless by-ways leading from his work into other regions of learning where he may find pleasure and improvement. There is one custom in vogue to-day among teachers in general, but particularly among art-teachers, that is not sufficiently considered in all its possibilities; it is the custom of demanding advance payment for instruction. Sometimes this term of payment extends over a period of two or three months. This makes it necessary on the part of the instructor who receives the money to have sufficient reserve fund always on hand to pay back the whole or any portion of such advance payment in case illness or sudden disability should render him incapable of fulfilling his contract. Yet how many teachers, think you, keep this very simple matter constantly before them? Manifestly it should be the first thought of the instructor to take care that he may be able to honor his contract; secondly, if he cannot do so, that he protect his patrons from loss through his disability.

To recapitulate, the main points, thus far, in this talk are :—

(*a*) You must take as great care of education as of material possession ; failing to do so, you become poorer.

(*b*) It is a business duty for you not merely to take your education to a high standard, but to keep it there.

(*c*) If you make business engagements for the future, you are duty bound, so far as you are able, to care for your health, that you may be permitted to meet them.

(*d*) Time and ability bring money; but money alone cannot bring you some of the richest pleasures of life; therefore do not set too great store by it. Learn to distinguish between Sufficient and Enough.

(*e*) Popularity and Worth are not always synonymous, but the one may exist with the other. Worth has fixed value. Popularity is accidental.

(*f*) The true business principle can be carried out in art as well as elsewhere.

In some respects the art-life is remunerative, but, as I have said before, it demands a long and faithful apprenticeship when there is little or no money earned, and when there is expense in many ways. I do not believe that over one per cent. of art instructors make an uncommonly good business venture of their education. The majority fail in the very beginning because they will not, or cannot, work years enough as learners to become instructors of the best kind. There is much truth in what Dr. Holmes says in "Elsie Venner": "A young man, using large endowments wisely and fortunately, may put himself on the level with the highest in the land in ten brilliant years of spirited, unflagging labor."

Impatience in the art-learner brings more harm

than good.　I fully believe the genius can make a way for himself; to the honest, determined workers who so love art that they feel impelled to seek the life-work in it one must say this,— unless you have sufficient financial help at hand to carry you over four or five years of study, you would better seek some employment that will allow you to earn sufficient to meet the expenses of living and of art education, and thus free you from the ruinous practice of trading in art before you have any art to trade with.　The modern art practicer can afford to wait, because if he really has talent for what he is doing his earning will in time compensate him for the enforced waiting.　He has not forever to struggle as his ancestors of two centuries ago.*

In fact, it is the apparent probability of considerable money return that brings so many into art.　They look upon the probable gains of teachers, composers, authors and all the rest with an

---

* Johann Bach, organist, received four bushels of grain as his annual emolument.　Even this failed him, and very justly he complained.　During one period of twenty-two years he received it once.

Nikolaus Ephraim Bach, a relative of Johann Bach, received an appointment to royalty as lackey, supervisor of pictures and statues, he shall be of use in music, cup bearer, organist, chief butler, instructor in music and painting, accountant to the abbess.　(See Philip Spitta's Life of Bach, Vol. 1, Bk. 1.)

It may be noted in this connection that among items of expense recorded by Beethoven, while in Vienna, is one of eight groschen (less than twenty cents) paid to Joseph Haydn, for lessons in strict counterpoint.　(See Grove's Dictionary of Music and Musicians, Vol. 1, p. 166, foot of first column.)

eye that favors this dearest wish. On the first arousing of their hope they do not calmly and justly consider how extensive are the concessions the brain-worker must make to his work, the work to the business, and the business to the actual demands of the people. But necessities arise one by one and throw the fortunes of the future into a constantly narrowing perspective. Let it be remembered that I am now speaking of business success, not of art success, for the one by no means promises the other. When work is done from the heart then the work is the pay. So thoughtlessly do people assume this or that line of activity, in which they imagine their friend or neighbor is succeeding, that one cannot but consider it a wise dispensation which brings about those fortunate failures, failures that are real successes because they take people away from what they are not fitted to perform, and thus may be the means of putting them where they can do well.

I have already said that I am now talking to you about art as a business; let me earnestly advise you to determine before you seek your daily bread in music, painting or literature to think seriously of these vital questions:—

(*a*) Have you any reasonable hope that with hard work and patience you can succeed as an honest workman in what you propose to do?

(*b*) Have you a just estimate of what financial gain
you may expect and are you able to wait until
you are able to earn before you try to earn?

(*c*) Are you willing to spend time and observation
in learning how to learn and then submit like a
faithful employé to those who guide you?

(*d*) In what do you place the most hope, in natural
ability or in hard work and plenty of it?

(*e*) Have you a just estimate of values, so that you
may estimate exactly the worth of your knowledge *to others?*

(*f*) Are you more strongly influenced in what you
undertake, to get money or to live a life of good
to yourself and to others; content to accept the
deed done as nine-tenths of the reward?

It is decidedly worth while to think of all these
things. They are powerful agents for or against
one's fortune. Success in art and literature is the
result of applying the most common-sense principles everywhere and at all times. Every beautiful
thought must have a common-sense basis or it
lacks value. Those flowers of literature, the fairy-
tales of Hans Christian Andersen, are loved and
valued because they find application in the homeliest
everyday life. Art life is just like one of these
sweet tales, a story of beautiful pictures full of
love for the good, heartful of kindness, rich in
beauty of such nature that it is content to abide in

any lowly place, be it the heart or home of an aspirant. By its presence it throws a glow of warmth about; yet underneath you will find that the picture is drawn not from fancy but from reason, that it is beautiful because it is sense adorned. It is the presence of beauty and truthful principle together, and that is art. Unless you enter art with a conviction that the world expects you to be a man or woman of sound sense and principle, no matter what you do, that it expects you to live and labor as well on the earth of actuality as in the clouds of probability, you will fail.

CHAPTER IV.

MUSICAL EDUCATION: BRAIN OR HAND?

The distinctive idea of an education is not to increase what a man knows, but to augment what a man is.—Rev. C. B. Hulbert, D.D.

You all know those two charming books by Louis Ehlert, found in most every musical library. Do you recall what he relates of himself in the chapter on Carl Taüsig in the volume, " From the Tone World ? " There is a grain of wisdom in it that well illustrates the theme we are talking about; let us read it together :—

" To reproduce and to create are by their very natures antitheses. Wherever they are found united, one of them must predominate, and although Shakespeare acted and Mendelssohn played the pianoforte, this was, in both cases, something accidental and secondary. I remember how, when in my youth, I went to study under Mendelssohn, he once asked me what form of art I thought of cultivating.

" ' I wish to become a pianoforte player,' said I.

" ' You don't contemplate composing ? ' he asked.

" ' I may think of it, but I don't believe I shall be able to accomplish it,' I replied.

" ' How can you submit to that ? ' he said."

You cannot long remain a student of art without learning that the mind as well as the hand must be educated. When you stand before a remarkable painting your first thought does not involuntarily turn to a consideration of the technical difficulty of the artist's work, but forcibly, fully, to its meaning. You search eagerly to discover his thought; you want to know what message he sends down to time in the painting before which you stand. You question the mind and soul of the artist, not his hand. Recognizing at once the beauty of his work you care more to know what he says in it than how he expresses himself; because the very first glance tells you if his expression is beautiful or not. There is in the National Gallery, in London, a painting by Girolamo del Pacchia, who was born about 1480; he is of the Sienese school. This painting is a " Madonna and child." The face of the mother is so full of resignation, of beauty that at once appeals to the heart, of beauty that is the lasting memorial of its own purity, that a beholder is entirely overcome by it. The deep and earnest meaning of the picture is so powerful that the critical tendency is at once crushed out of being and one is left deep in admiration for what the artist put into the sweet womanly face before us. This power of art is strange, inexplicable; I fear I cannot express it to you. One must have experienced it. The lesson it conveys, however, is this: you must look not to the means but to the meaning of art if you would know its true worth. If experience in the presence of some work of art or of literature teaches you this in a forcible way you will draw instinctively this conclusion: if, as a student of art, I hope to produce a work of value, its worth and my worth will be judged by what I put into it, not by my way of doing; if I spend my life as an art educator my worth will also be judged by what I put into it; hence the more there is of me the more I can express. Hence I must see how much there is of me, for of what there is I make my future. It is only such consideration as this that will turn you in the right direction. In travel, so in art; know before you start in what direction you must go, and never lose your East. "When a traveler arrives at a strange city, or is overtaken by night, or by a storm, he takes out his compass and learns which way is the East, or Orient. Forthwith all the cardinal points,—east, west, north, south,—take their true places in his mind, and he is in no danger of seeking for the sunrise or the pole-star in the wrong quarter of the heavens. *He orients himself.*" * So you lead in the art-life by

---

* Horace Mann.

having once learned its truth and beauty, and keeping them ever before you that you may orient yourself.

You all know how common among us is that class of self-styled instructor who can in reality train neither the brain nor the hand. Their motive for invading where they do not belong is plainly expressed in all they do. In nine-tenths of cases the amount of endeavor they expend could be used honestly to more purpose. In art they are not honestly employed, because they have taken no pains to inquire into the nature of what they do, nor the necessary qualification for fulfilling it to a purpose. At the outset, therefore, you see how false is the position of any one who is not so impressed with the nobility of his toil as to do his best for it in all ways and at all times. We have, heretofore, spoken of the business principle in art; is it not evident to you that no principle whatever is at the bottom of the motive which leads one to seek gain in offering himself to do what he cannot? The best education you can get in art is that which makes something of you. Then you will know what it means to guide others. "If it is not in your power to make yourself what you would be, how can you expect to have the moulding of others?" By applying common-sense always you will not fail to see that the hand depends for what it can do upon the mind; that without mind-value the work of the hand can have no great worth. If you will look back and trace the lives of the men whom the world calls great you will see that the work of their hands was dictated to them in the training of the mind, and that the purer the mind the greater the worth. We have a warm place in the heart for Beethoven and Raphael Santi and Michael Angelo, because they put a great meaning in all they did. They were wise enough to use the power they had *thereby to gain more*. When you set out to acquire an art education you simply erect an altar at which the world expects you to worship. You worship in accordance with what you are, hence strive continually to be more. You will learn in the school-room of experience how to execute your ideas. Let your thoughts be turned toward getting more ideas of the best kind. With these ideas you build. Throughout your life as an artist you will find that the brain gives to the hand the idea, that is to say, the raw material with which it is to work. From this statement, simple as it is, you cannot fail to conclude that the efforts of those who endeavor to gain a technical education out of proportion with the mind education that accompanies it, are founded upon the most senseless basis, for it is the mind that inspires the hand. Dexterity with the brush on the canvas, with the fingers on the key-board, is of no value in itself. The mind must inspire something for the hand to do, then worth comes. With the chisel one man spends his life hewing paving stones ; another brings forth from the marble figures that seem to lack nothing but breath to make them human.

[It may be fitting for me to say here that you are not to consider your art-life passed to no purpose unless you occupy a high place. To you the question should never assume that aspect; ask yourself how well you may fill the place you are fitted for, by the constant exercise of your greatest endeavor and judgment. In life,—and art is nothing more nor less than a phase of life,—worth is not relatively measured; it is absolute in every individual case, and is computed only in respect to individual powers.]

The world accepts men and women wherever it can find them; what it wants of them is their earnestness, and it wants that earnestness well directed. By a just law, none the less to be respected because there are seen here and there glaring instances of its non-fulfilment, those of much ability fill the higher places, and those of less, lower in proportion. Life settles things justly—by which I mean that, as a rule, striving men find their level, and the question is not how great a place does one fill, but, how greatly does one fill it. In every phase of art-life there are great themes; earnestness is everywhere, frivolity nowhere. For a while your playing of pretty airs will win you listeners, but if you are discovered to be lower in mind and nature than the task you assume, the guiding hands of those about you will surely lead you to the place you deserve. You will be remembered only while you are seen. It matters not how little may be your ability, you cannot afford to be an art-despoiler; you cannot afford to be content with educational veneer when the solid timber is to be had for the work of cutting it. If the young men and women who assume the art-life would remember that they make themselves in it just as other people do in walks of life that appear less rosy to the poetic vision of the young art-enthusiast, there would be more earnest determination and less sentimental inactivity. Art does not offer a life of exquisite dream in a perfumed atmosphere; it is hard work and common-sense in the home of the beautiful; and the task is all the more difficult because the theme is rich and varied.

As plant life will not thrive in an inch of loam spread over a deep layer of gravel, so will no one succeed in the desired self-development who sets a great deal of hope in a little endeavor.   Unless art is made a useful working-tool in life you cause it to miss its purpose.   You may be sure there is much in it, for true and noble lives have been lived in its service.   But they have been lives of deep and earnest thought; lives in which the heart and mind have sought busily to find work for the hands, not mere idle playing for these hands.   Did you ever think of all there is in the word "education?" *e* and *duco*, to lead out something from within, the ability of leading from the mind properties of value. Knowledge is the raw material worked over in the mind; of itself it is never education.   There is no phrase in our language so many times wrongly applied as "well-educated;" in many instances of its application it refers to no education whatever, but to knowledge-gathering; and that is quite another matter.   Knowledge and experience work over slowly in the mind; that is why the art education is a slow process.   One must smile, involuntarily, at those aspirants for sure and easy honors who turn for them to music, painting, literature and the sciences.   They find that maturity does not come in a moment; but even this thought comes only after they have tried in vain now one art now another, searching always for the sudden acquisition of a desired possession that another has gained only after the greatest labor.   Why true men in any walk of life are not spoiled by the success that comes to them is because they know how impossible it is to escape being what they are after the years of thoughtful labor they have done. You will conceive more clearly the exact meaning of art when you know that a knowledge of drawing and a keen eye for color are only a tiny step toward being a painter; you will conceive art better when you know that a technical command of the pianoforte key-board is a small item in the equipment of a musician.   Art-life is a concentration of all the happenings of a lifetime, of knowledge, inspiration, conception, reproduction, happiness, sorrow, hope and fear.   All of these and many others have their influence.

You make a great deal of art, you think it a rare privilege to experience its phases.   That is right. But art is only one form of life, of which labor in the fields is another, and both are lived to the same end.   In idealizing your occupation do not scorn the doings of another who works in a more lowly place.   While you think upon the elevation of your calling and the humbleness of his he may be doing his task better than you do yours.

In art, hand-training means little if there has not been much other training with it.   The farmer plows the ground not to show his neighbor what a straight furrow he can cut, *but to make something grow.* What is known in music as technical power is of volatile nature compared with what comes from the productive worth of solid education. Great skill in drawing fine lines is nothing if the mind cannot conceive some application for them. The technical skill cannot live, cannot be transmitted nor bequeathed; but the conceived and executed work is the property of all times.

CHAPTER V.

MUSIC IN AMERICA.

A mesure que le peuple prend plus d'intérêt aux événements plus ou moins historiques, il puise de nouveaux sujets pour ses productions poétiques dans ceux qui font le plus d'impression sur son sentiment et son imagination.—Léon Sichler.

There is nothing more fascinating than to trace the dawn of literature among a people. Man, alive with wonder, stands before nature, as a child filled with astonishment. He cannot conceive what he beholds. By slow degrees he translates the happenings of nature into speech, and his first act is to do it poetically; showing, thereby, that beauty exists as well in him as about him. The sun warms, the earth produces, the river flows; he deifies them; calls the sun father; the earth mother; the river a brave courser. The plain is to him a world; he rides across it a monarch. Then he reasons with himself and concludes that, as he has tamed his horse and is able to support himself in his surroundings, why may he not conquer nature yet further? He wonders what he may force the soil to yield, and to satisfy his curiosity he works upon it. Nature makes him wait; he conceives it in this manner: first, he must wait a few days, then many more days, a whole season, a longer time, then the soil rewards his labor. Now nature has conquered him by allowing him to be the conqueror. Then he is thankful and sings to nature; he weaves about her fanciful stories, full of rich imaginings. The earth, the river and the mountain are his people. The earth is a goddess, mother of children; he is one of them; the river is another, it travels into foreign countries, conquering as it goes; it wins strength from many tributaries which become its army. In the thunder, the child of the early world hears an angry voice; in the lightning, he sees the flash of fiery eyes; darkness is a pall laid over the earth that it may slumber; light is a summons to activity. So height and depth, soft and hard, warmth and cold, do not appeal to him in the stern force of reality until long after he has endowed them with poetic characteristics, god-qualities of strength and rigid demand.

Thus the peasant of the early world is at once a child of the soil and the father of poets. He sings of the forces of nature; teaches his songs to his children down through many generations, and thus sends his first thoughts of wonder to distant times. His first trial is for self-reliance; that won he begins to study his own strength and to measure it with the strength of nature. He soon learns what the seasons require of him and what he may force from them ; he finds strength in the current of the winding river and subdues it, makes it obey the guiding of his hand.   He recognizes a god in the fury of the sea, in the fury of war, in the uncertainty of chance.   He never lacks the most marvellous means to ascribe a cause; he acknowledges no impossibility in the weaving of his songs and legends, his epics and his sagas.   After he has looked for motive in nature he turns and looks for motive within himself; he looks upon his strength and weakness in right or wrong and as he has sung of nature he sings of them.   All the time he is learning, he is providing his children with a rich heritage and that heritage is oral literature, the parent of every beautiful conception of art and letters to this day.

Thus did the wonderful literature of Greece take its beginning ; thus in Russia did the moujic make his byline and tell of the enemy-forces of nature. In the mountains he has a hero, Sviatogor ; in the river Volkof he has another ; in adventure he has Volga, the warrior hero ; in Mikoula, the hero of the soil and of the people.   In every phase of life he deifies, ascribes strength to a wonderful being whom he does not see nor know, simply that he may be able to offer himself some explanation of what he does not understand.   It was the peasant of the

North, the South and the East that forced literature to spring up so richly in western Europe. He taught his songs and legends to other peoples, scattered the seed of his rich imaginings in other lands; it sprouted, became a hardy plant and will never cease its growth. Not the dawn of literature alone but the dawn of art is found in these mind-buildings of the night of time. In fables and folk-tales, in epic and saga, man has ever proclaimed himself a great scene-painter, a picture builder of wonderful power; the coloring is vivid, maybe not always logical, but always rich. Harmony pervades the parts even though they be rudely joined. There is always meaning, though it may be over-beautified. It is the extravagance of rich coloring in the mind-pictures of early literature that seizes upon us. The modern mind is surprised at it because it has been trained to be economical, to develop the theme for all there is in it; we have come to learn that development of subject, in art and letters, is the greatest task that can be imposed on the skilful artist. The byline and the saga do not so develop; at every turn they teem with new beauty, with greater magnificence and increased splendor. The extravagant imagination that opens a Russian byline with the marriage of a young prince to a frog is as nothing compared with the ever increasing wonder of the picture. The frog-wife is a most beautiful woman; this the prince learns, and in his haste ever to keep her so, he burns the frog-skin. As a punishment he loses her. He seeks her amid immense difficulties to be rewarded at length with this enigma: He finds her in the keeping of a sorcerer; a so-called Baba-Iaga tells him this; the sorcerer is Kostschey the Immortal, whom it is most difficult to find. The prince, ere he can regain his beautiful young wife, must take the life of Kostschey; his death is at the point of a needle, the needle in an egg, the egg in a duck, the duck in a hare, the hare in a chest, the chest at the top of a lofty oak tree; and this tree Kostschey guards as if it were the apple of his eye. With a single sweep of the brush on the canvas the painter shows us that the prince fails not to outwit the crafty sorcerer. No difficulties that he can bring together in his story are insurmountable at the desired moment and in the twinkling of an eye.

[All the tales of Scheherazade are as wonderful in their effects of instantaneous change. The fascination of following the intricate windings of her recitals lies in the character of rapid transition to which there is united remarkable color. The Arabian Nights will always be read with the keenest delight; and the stories of the Three Calenders, of Sinbad the Sailor, of Beder, Prince of Persia, and the stories of Zobeide and of Amine will ever be delightful pictures in the temple of the memory].

Amid such wonders did the art and letters of the old world have their beginning. In the Kalevala, the Iliad, the Epics of India and the Byline of Russia modern art and letters find their parentage. There is antiquity in them; the wonders of the early world, of man the peasant, of man the warrior are held there in crystallization. They fascinate us because they bring remote time to the scrutiny of the present. Try as we will we cannot break away from the art and story of antiquity, nor from the art and story of the old world, because they are strong in the humanity of their birthright. The art of nations is but a phase of this art of the world; a crystallization of certain peculiar surroundings of a group of people. Individualized by their manners and customs, by geographical situation and climatic influence, by their individual strength as a nation and by their place among other peoples, they give a coloring and a force to their productions that is a true expression of all their life. In the old world the art of nations may be traced to remote times and the cumulating influence of centuries is recognized in its every feature to-day. It has direct ancestry which is a possession of great worth.

Everywhere, influence from this side and from that
has come in, has left its trace, but only in the way
of a modification. The direct result of a people's
unity is not lost or annihilated by such outside
bearings. This unity of a people is the strongest
of all factors in the coloring of its thought. The
varying phases of art in Europe are due, and cor-
respond exactly to the varying phases of the history
of the nations. What is typical of one alone is
due to the privacy of its life. What is common to
all is due to the great power of the humanizing
influence that has been working upon the family
of nations for centuries. Individual traits are as
commonly found among races as among the
children of a household; nurtured in one home
and under one guidance they, nevertheless, preserve their individuality.

The causes that have combined to make the art
and literature of Europe the logical outcome of
its past teach us that every nation must seek its
intellectual ancestry in the same way. America is
a young nation of no past; we are not a people of
epic and legend; we have not the rich heritage of
an antiquity made brilliant by active minds strug-
gling in the wonder-world. Our poets feed not on
a past, but ever busy in the present, they are making a rich history for the future. Our mountains
and rivers were not sung of before to-day by our

own race ; our warriors are men of our own time. Our old men tell very modern tales to the grand-children.   In one sense there is nothing against us in all this but we must not forget that it colors our intellectual out-putting.   As a nation sprung from the seeds of the old world we turn thither in our thoughts as sons and daughters who have gone out from the home.   An offshoot of the countries of the old world, we find its history our own ; with us, however, it does not thrive so well because it is not surrounded by the attending results of the antiquity of which it is a part, but to offset this loss it breathes a freer, a purer air, it has acting upon it the influences of a unique present.   While in itself our art-practice would starve if fed upon nothing but home-association it constantly appeals to our students to seek inspiration in the domains of our rightful ancestry.   We are a conglomerate people ; and thereby we appeal to more history than any other nation of the world.   But this rich ancestry that we can accept as our own is a great care, for it is a priceless possession only when we have developed it.   Inspiration must be well-directed or it will yield nothing.   What richer heritage can befall any nation than the history of the nations that have made it a people and the life-phases of the human family whose joy and sorrow, whose struggle and victory are dear to everyone?   A nation's struggle for freedom, its loyalty to truth and right, its home-history are dear to all. Why? Because all these things appeal to the heart and the heart is one in all mankind. The true ancestry of America is the rich past of the old world, but we find it mingling with one powerfully acting factor, namely, an independent present. It is a commercial present that seems forgetful whence it came. We are yet striving very eagerly to make art and bank-accounts meet on a common level. But American art is slowly gaining. A literature once well founded, our art-ascendency is a certainty; for it is worthy of remark that in the intellectual history of all nations, art follows letters.

We have seen that the art-history of the world is made up of the art-history of individual nations, and that these nations are characterized by their surroundings, their manners and customs, by their relationships. In just the same way a nation's art tendency, a nation's intellectualism, are the result of individual attainment. The history of a nation rests in the hands of its units; as in politics and finance, so in art. Each of these units has not to think of the duty of all the rest, but to mind its business. It is an admirable thing to do, and one should try to do it well. Reducing our terms of enquiry to one lower place we find that individual qualification depends on two factors, ability and training; or, in other words, on individuality developed by education. It is only a serious consideration of the question of art-education that can give a nation a place in art-practices. At the present state of our history we are not *as a people* conscious of the educational value of art; the amateur is constantly becoming more numerous, but he is playful with art, he does not regard it seriously. When art is adopted as a means for livelihood it is too soon abandoned for money. A few remain true to their calling, these typify the nation and it is for the influence they exert that no educational good be denied them. In time all governments see the truth of this and give some recognition to art-study, feeling content that if the general learner assumes no eminence there may come now and then one who shall be the nation's glory. To produce great works of art there must be food for the inspiration, and that food must be delved for. "The New World keeps the imagination on plain and scanty diet, compared to the rich traditional and historic food which furnishes the banquet of the Old World." If means are not at hand they must be sought. Art is rich in its out-putting when it is earnestly followed. A desire to vaunt the individual self before real worth has been attained is the cause of much of the art-poverty from which we suffer. The desire to popularize art cannot

succeed, for great art can never become popular.
I am reminded of what Goethe said to Eckermann:
" Dear friend, I will tell you, in confidence, something that will, in the future, aid you in the comprehension of many things, and which will serve
you all your life. My works can never become
popular. He who thinks to the contrary, and who
strives to make them so, is working for a fruitless
cause. They are not written to the mass, but to
those, who, longing for and searching for that for
which I have hoped and striven, walk in the way
that I have walked." *

Art must be infinitely greater than the people,
else it will never be recognized as art remarkable.
The so-called popular art is only the pool left by
the splashing of the waves about the coast; it
is not the wondrous, powerful movement of the
ocean's breast. It is the faintest echo of the sound.
A musical nation is not one that seizes with avidity
every new song of the day, but one that now and
then produces a leader. That is possible with us.
But it means much labor, just as the symphony
means years of musical art without a symphony.
A rich art-history in America, as in any other
nation, means the unappreciated labor of many;
it means the presence of the specialist, the force

---

* Goethe et la musique, ses jugements, son influence, les œuvres qu'il a
inspirées. Adolphe Jullien. Paris: 1880.

of a literature, deep study on the part of a few of the violent history of the world and of the human race; it means a ready sympathy with the joys and grievances of mankind; it means privation and suffering ere the goal is won; it means that to possess an art-history comparable with that of the old world America must labor, suffer persistently, strive for it, and this labor, this suffering must be felt by those who are willing to live for the purpose of bequeathing a worthy heritage to a people.

The value of art to a nation is its power to civilize, to make better and more tolerant. It betokens an elevation of thought, a nobility of purpose that are beyond value as exemplars. No nation can get it at a lower price than others have had to pay for it. This means that in the earnestness of the individual art-practicers a nation puts all its trust.

There are American composers whose names would do honor to these pages. Be so far willing to meet the new with a warm heart as to give them your thought and attention. I assure you, many of them deserve it. You can only know the beauty of your garden by taking a walk in it.

CHAPTER VI.

THE SPECIALIST.

Un mortel bien faisant approche de Dieu même.   RACINE.

Great deeds must be worked for, hoped for, died for, now as in the past.
      SCHUMANN.

I have already said to you that one of the best signs of art progress is the appearance of art-specialists. Of this progress the elementary specialist is the keystone. We teach too indiscriminately. Any one who knows something immediately seeks another who knows less, to whom he would be preceptor. In this attempt there is plainly evidenced an abandon that is alarming. You know or will soon learn that nothing is apparently easier, but, in reality, more difficult, than the task of initiating one in special education. It appears easy because you feel so positive of your knowledge; it is really difficult, because a product of nature cannot be moulded and adapted without great skill and judgment.

The elementary instructor is usually an accident. Having entered the lists for a greater prize and failed, he discontentedly takes what he can get, generally it is not much. He is seldom a satisfactory quantity either to himself or to those with whom he forms relationships. The reason for this is found in the manner in which he came to his station. It was unexpected even to himself. I cannot conceive how it is that any one can begin the study of art without having in view a definite object, or, at least, an object relatively definite. The traveler has usually a destination. Later on, conditions and the first developments of the education may somewhat modify the first formed plan. Just so, what the traveler sees by the way may cause him to vary his journey; still a generally definite object is always entertained. The traveler, no matter how far and wide he wanders, finds no place so sweet to him as the fatherland, the home; he may love to wander about the world, but a gravity of irresistible power is forever urging him whence he came. So, too, the one who enters the art world loves to wander in it far and wide, to study its phases great and small, to gather wisdom by roaming far from home. You know how great is the walk of life. One cannot be at home everywhere in it. You know how necessary it is to take up a home, to develop it, to live in and about it, to show how much one can do in and about it by wisdom brought from afar. It is characterized by you and by it are you characterized.

Thus let us regard it that every one should find for himself a place in art-work, and exert himself to do the most therein. If the chosen place be high or low the credit, in the end, will be only in accordance with how the work has been done. In the end it is the absolute, not the relative result, that is considered. The silent thought has a sonorous echo.*

Let us now talk of the specialist in elementary art. However exalted you may be, in fancy or in reality, I think you will agree with me, before this talk is ended, that you owe much, both in what you are and in what you do, to small beginnings. No one needs more special and general education than the instructor. Having to make a mansion of the mind how carefully must he labor that everything may be well and solidly founded. His work is on the line of employment which teaches him that more skill and judgment are required to set the diamond than to build a wall of stone. Attention to little things, absolute certainty in considering them and in tracing their relationships for others, teach him that no thought is too insignificant

---

* Saintine has said this in "Picciola": "La pensée muette a un écho sonore."

5

to entertain.   There is no field of art-teaching in which an extensive general education is of more practical value than in this of which we speak; yet the special training must be none the less extensive.   Comparison, illustration and connection, when they are constantly and carefully made for the young student between what he does and what lies just beyond the confines of his work, will aid so much in making him a careful observer at all times that nothing can adequately represent the value of their suggestiveness.   It is hint-giving in early life that shapes the thought-harvest of after years.   No one in art-education has greater opportunity for hint-giving than the first teacher.   And further than this no one should be more capable to do it, by nature and training, than he.   Hence, I recognize in the elementary specialist one who willingly occupies a world too small for what he can do; and the wisdom of his choice is not at fault nor is it ludicrous, for who is not too great for the place he occupies is too small for it.   Some of the best gifts of literature embody in the simplest form the most profound teachings.   One may instance the fairy-tales of Hans Christian Andersen. Such writing is truly bringing down fire from above.   Knowledge so gathered, its items arranged, tested, given minute application and logical sequence, is the result of wide research brought to bear upon a single object. I can conceive of no more difficult line of inquiry for you to follow than that of the specialist; at the same time you can rise but very little above the level of all ordinary musicians if you refuse to concentrate your thought, not only upon one subject, but upon one phase of a subject. It is in this, especially, that peculiar natural fitness is demanded; mere choice to become an orchestral conductor means nothing unless the desire is the unconquerable result of special talent forcing you that way; nor can you become the most noted instructor of first-year students unless natural fitness makes you desire to work on that level after having spent much time in inquiry above and about it.

We will talk about the elementary specialist; perhaps some of you do not yet clearly picture to yourselves how rare a personality it must be that is adapted to such a place. That one may encounter hundreds of elementary teachers in the course of a day's search is not to be denied. The accidental nature of their station is amusing. Assuming to be well-trimmed, symmetrical trees in a park, they are in reality but straggling scrub in a thicket. Yet the accident of their station is not surprising, for nothing is more difficult of attainment than the object they are supposed to pursue. Outside of the special art-knowledge necessary as a raw material with which to work one must possess the faculty of judging quickly and correctly every personality that is met with; one must have always ready the happy faculty of making a picture of life from little hints seen and heard now and again; all these to be remembered over long periods, if necessary, and put together, at the proper time, bit by bit, mosaic-wise. I would have this ideal elementary instructor a fond student of human-nature away from his lesson hours, and I should expect him to learn much in the great world that he would apply in the little one. He should be full of active sympathy in art and out of it, hopeful himself and hope-inspiring always. This and all else about the man or woman should be the outcome of a rich and highly endowed nature; it cannot come to any one by the careful observance of rules.

What should you know about your students? Here are a few hints, find others for yourself: You should know their natural qualification, their strong and weak points, how they are affected by diffidence or fear, what is their home-life, what training and influence have been brought to bear upon them, are they trying to create an art-atmosphere in a home that favors or antagonizes it, how do they work, how do they spend leisure hours, what is their life in and out of music, what physical strength or weakness have they, where particularly do they encounter difficulties, what degree of conscientiousness do they put in the work they do for you, is their ambition well-founded, how do work and ambition compare, what is the strength and tendency of taste, how do they work through the year, how do they take discouragement, what has nature done for them, what can education do with the natural ability, what motive lies back of their ambition? and so on through a thousand changes that I need not ring.

In art education the elementary instruction is directed not upon children alone but to learners of every age. Hence all phases of human nature are at one time or another wrought upon by the instructor of first principles, and what does he but plant the same variety of seed in an endless variety of soils? Need any one ask why it flourishes not the same in all? Nothing is more difficult in all education than to be consistently clear and simple, never once anticipating what has not been taught and still making free use of comparative means. Perhaps you would like to try this for yourselves? Then I suggest that you explain in the simplest terms to the members of your household the individual character of the two songs of Schubert: "*Der Tod und das Mädchen*" and "*Das Wandern*," for instance; then compare and contrast them;

remember that you are to use the fewest possible technical terms nor draw too freely your means from performance. Some variations of like experience will teach you that to thrust knowledge upon all alike, indiscriminately, is a very easy matter, to bring it just within the student's reach is not so easy, and lastly, to put it just so far above him that he may benefit by climbing after it is most difficult of all.

I would advise you to become observing students of educational methods in any kind of school, art or not; you will gather experience of value, because in most everything but art,—how best to teach,—is a question granted the most careful study. From the kindergarten to the most special technological schools educators are constantly experimenting as to the best way of helping students to help themselves; but in art the schoolmaster still falls asleep every afternoon, his spectacles slip over his nose, and his scholars all play with truant minds. Visit schools, question school-children, read educational treatises and determine that if no one will teach you how to be as worthy an educator in art as men become out of art, you will teach yourself. There must yet be founded a school for the training of educators in art, or art cannot maintain its educational level with other subjects. Art-teachers spend too much time undoing each other's work; the students themselves who go from one teacher to another have to undergo the *unwinding process* too much; this process has become so general that your new student is most of all interested in what change of educational diet he must be put upon, and if it so chances that you do not think it necessary to change the course of his work he begins, at once, to doubt your ability to manage his case. And his conclusion is not altogether ill-founded; even his very slight experience has taught him that art educators do not work to each other's interest; the reason whereof is that while one works earnestly for art itself a dozen or so of his neighbors work three times as earnestly for the money they think there is in it.

I feel certain that it is best to advise you to turn very careful attention to special work in art, always remembering it is the special training that requires the most general education. And I can likewise say to you that there is no branch of art more in need of specially trained instructors than elementary art; no field has greater nor more important requirements for them nor will any field better repay one for earnest, unselfish devotion in its behalf. No other branch of art-study will give more return in all ways than this. At the same time it offers unlimited hard work and comparatively little recognition; however, I do not expect your course to be altered because of these two conditions. Art, being unselfish can hardly be expected to pay. You must study, not so much what is in demand, as what ought to be in demand.

What can one say to those of you who assume this place in art? First of all this—the most precious reward you can receive for your labor is the work done so that you may feel proud of it. The best legacies you can leave your students are the well-trained, studious habit, respect for doing any task great or small, reverence for art and a thankfulness to God for whatever talent He has given. It is a delicate matter to lead the mind, and the way it is done makes one shudder at the crime. There are countless ways that you may urge your students onward, as well out of art as in it; this is why you should have knowledge and experience besides that of your specialty. Perhaps you may nourish in one a fond taste for reading, or you may help on an ability to accomplish something in another field; do it, if your best judgment says it is well. Be interested in what has interest for your learners; they will like you better for it, will trust you farther, do more for you. When one is cold, do not say to him: Dance, hadji, and thou wilt get warm. There is no consolation in that. You will learn that encouragement is the best of all discipline; at the same time you must know how to command, keep to your point and show as much determination in having the uncongenial task properly done as you do sympathetic encouragement in the most pleasing phase of study. Put ideas into all you say; that is, always say something that your students know will be worth listening to. "Bigness is not greatness, nor fury force" has not fitter application than here. You will find that, as a general rule, good results follow good sense, and you will also come to have more faith in understanding than in method.

The specialist is one among many workers all to the same end. One cuts down the tree, another trims it, another takes it to the mill, another saws it, another planes it, another cuts it into veneers, another introduces them into fine cabinet work, another gives them polish and another finds use for the work when it is done. It is so in all things.

CHAPTER VII.

THE AMATEUR.

Eyeryone admits the value of application, but very few are aware how its force is wasted by diffusion : it is like a volatile essence in a bottle without a cork.—JAMES PAYN.

The amateur is a student who is not compelled by fortune or the lack of it to call himself a professional follower of what he enjoys as an avocation. Whoever, voluntarily, follows out in art-study a particular line of thought, who is drawn to it by an inborn love, who puts good into it and gets good from it, is a valuable person both to self and to society. We are fairly judged by our avocations. When that avocation elevates the mind and gives exquisite pleasure it adds lustre to one's life, it makes life more than every-day existence, it offers byways leading from the highway that are cool, refreshing and rest-giving. It makes one hope longingly for the pleasure that can be had when a day's toil is done. The lowest employment is less repulsive when it is done by one who knows that in a few hours he may have the pleasure of doing something more akin to his feelings and desires. Lack of fortune may make us very poor in the riches of the pocket, but it cannot lay its hand on the riches of the mind. One thinks of Sherburne W. Burnham, the astronomer, of Arminius Vambèry, the poor youth and philologist who trudged all over Asia, of Schliemann's fortunes in the fascinating autobiographical pages of " Ilios." Two of these men were more than amateurs, nevertheless, in the early days of their striving they did not suspect how brilliantly their flickering light would one day burn. In the world of the amateur there is immense possibility.

One does not recognize as an amateur every villainous dabbler in art and science; nine-tenths of these are art-despoilers, who learn to paint and to play because it is fashionable; who patronize this and that æsthetic intellectual theme because they think they should, doing as gracefully as the poor Asiatic servant, who deemed it proper in him to copy his master and wear a cravat; the reform was incomplete insomuch that he continued to wear it anywhere between the proper place and the back of the neck. A true amateur is that gifted person who does not make a life activity of what he has ability to perform; he has all the gifts and ability of his professional brother, but, having no need to apply them as constantly, lacks his experience; as compensation for this he preserves a freshness in his avocation that would be entirely lost to him if

it were a calling.   He is not less studious because
he wishes to follow a line of thought in an unpro-
fessional way; on the contrary, he puts thought
and patient inquiry in all he does; he has his
plans, his reasons, his considerations all carefully
outlined and followed as best he can with what
means and time he can command.   I think it is
Dr. Holmes who says that his literary activity was
carried on for thirty years coincidently with the
dry teaching of anatomy, and while the literary
outcome of that period smacks in nothing of the
amateur, it may in every respect be regarded as an
ideality for amateur activity.   It is furnishing to
others good and pleasure in the hours one need
not devote to bread-winning.

The amateur is in every sense a missionary.   He
carries the light of many beautiful stars to those
who, unaided, could not see them.   The good he
may do in the home, and consequently in society,
is immeasurable.   He is the Prometheus who carries the fire of genius to warm mortals; yet he is not
punished; his duty thus done is generous in its
reward.   There is much peculiar to the life of the
professional man that forbids him bringing all his
discovery of truth and beauty directly to the
people; he needs one other who will study his
ways in detail; who will spend time in unravelling
and discovering to others what he himself conceives

as a whole; there must be a class who, for the love of it, will take a little of the great store of art and science and knowledge and carry it where otherwise it could never go. Between the man of no natural gift, the mere worker who copies his master, and the divinely gifted one whose mind has been abundantly enriched by God, there is too great a distance; nature will not tolerate the intense monopoly of the one nor the extreme want of the other. Hence, between these distant phases of intellectual ability there must come in one who, having some of the ability of the one, can sympathize with the want of the other. That is how the amateur may be accounted for; he stands between and explains; he interprets, he makes clear that his own teaching may serve as a guide to those who cannot trust themselves alone.

You all have not failed to observe in the art-study you have already done, that the easy way in which we use the word "professional," the indiscriminate way in which it is applied, results simply from a lack of perception in a fitness of title to persons. We do not yet live in times so enlightened that every one thinks as he should for himself; nor are we, as a people, unsusceptible to the glittering enticements of humbug. The hen still soars with the eagle. It thrives because it is so well cared for. If by any means it were possible to take from every intellectual pursuit the self-styled professors whose only claim to their office is their assumption, we would behold such a weeding out as should cause us to wonder how the few able ones ever succeed at all, staggering as they labor under the immense encumbrance of so many parasites. Then if we would look closely at each individual member of this parasitic mass we would further discover that very few possess the makings of the true amateur. Hence, we may conclude regarding art-followers, thus :—

The true professional follower is one endowed by nature and training for his office; he gives his time and thought to the work, and his life is colored and influenced by it almost completely.

The true amateur is one endowed by nature and, to a certain extent, by training, for his avocation; he does not give all his time and thought to it, but his life is colored and influenced by it to a certain extent.

The would-be professional may be (*a*) one who has the gifts of the amateur, little experience and insufficient training; (*b*) one who has no fitness for the work he undertakes, plenty of assumption, and a keen thought for money. Three-quarters of the influence exerted by the professional and amateur is necessary to combat the evil influence of these two classes of presumptive workers, the one an unripe fruit, the other no fruit at all.

No one will find a warmer welcome in art than the well-endowed amateur; he is earnest, sympathizes with the artist, conceives his designs though he may not be able to execute them. He cannot be honored too much. By patient study he recognizes the worth and value of art production; he is not overhasty in his judgment, because he makes it a practice to think before he speaks, he does not despise what he does not understand. Having sympathy with the beautiful, he finds that it brightens the prosaic hours of daily life. Learning from the application of its means how it adds pleasure to his own life, he soon divines that he may cause it to give pleasure to the life of others, and he finds the phases and poses of his statue to be without limit. I have in mind two amateurs in the musical art, both of whom you well know; the one, Fanny Mendelssohn, sister of the composer, the other, Frau von Genzinger, that delightful, noble woman, with whom we become acquainted in the Letters of Joseph Haydn. On the other hand, the presumptive art-follower is as readily recognized by what he has not. Mendelssohn has drawn a pleasing portrait in one of his early letters: "With L——, too, I get on famously. He is very pleasing, and the most *dilletante* of all the *dilletanti* I ever met. He knows everything by heart, and plays wrong basses to them all; he is

only deficient in arrogance, for with all his unde-
niable talent, he is very modest and retiring."

If you will look carefully through the bibliogra-
phy of any one topic you will be surprised to learn
how much skillful, indispensable literary work is
done by the true amateur; done voluntarily, cheer-
fully and well. He generally undertakes to initiate
those who cannot find for themselves the means for
taking up the first weight. He lessens the burden
by dividing it, which is truly a worthy task if it be
done unselfishly. Viewed from another point, the
amateur is the true patron of art. He judges,
leads the public mind by informing it, tells what to
see in art, and is in a general sense the interpreter
between the artist and the people. These three
factors, artist, amateur and public, always stand at
the same relative distance one from the other, and,
as a natural consequence, the higher the plane
reached by the artist, correspondingly high will the
amateur elevate himself, pulling the public up after
him. Thus art elevation and art degeneracy are
felt through the entire social fabric.

You, students of art, assume a professional
standing, because you have given to yourselves and
to others sufficient guarantee of your ability to do
so. The world of the amateur may be open to
you in two ways, first, you may, as an instructor,
be called upon frequently to outline and conduct

the education of a gifted person who does not care to enter the active professional life; secondly, you may, for your own part, desire to take up, in a similar way, studies apart from your own. The first relationship will require you to be selective, to the end that the learner may not have unnecessarily to labor in the details that are of use only to the purely professional student; in the second relationship you will look upon the very result you are bringing about in another, and will, if you be a man of thought, see where you may give and take to the greatest advantage. You will learn and teach that the presumptive ones fail to do any good work because they do not place their values relatively and justly. In the art life or out of it you will find that, of itself, knowledge is not education, more than a handful of seed is a garden. In either sphere thought must be made healthy by labor and labor made happy by thought. Knowledge is what we gather, what we pick up here and there, either because it pleases us or because it offers interest. Education is what all this does for us; it is what it makes of us. As soon as it turns its notice upon you, the world asks at once what motive shines through your activity. Only after this does it turn to look at your station.

CHAPTER VIII.

CHILDREN.

We are very near God at both ends of the life journey; one can see this deep down in the eyes of children and of old men. I wish to devote a talk to children for this reason; as the small beginning is a strong factor in every affair of life so the beginning of life,—childhood,—is the most wonderful time; then speed is gathered and direction taken.   All the world's affairs of half a century hence are to be managed by the children of to-day. They are important then.   Should we not pay heed to the inheritors of so much ?   They will make us, whether we will or not. " Bard or hero cannot look down on the word or gesture of a child." Art is possible because a number of men and women devote life to it, make it their work and their care; when they are done with it others take it up. As childhood is the apprentice-time of life, so it is the apprentice-time in life's affairs. Now if we admit that art may be taught to children or that in early years the first steps in art are to be taken, it seems that our duty as artists of one school and another is very grave toward the young. I do not picture them in sombre seriousness because of what may devolve upon them, but in pleasurable anticipation, upon which wisdom must be engrafted. That is where the duty lies. I do not think that the thunderbolt is necessary as a factor of discipline in child-life. Hence I do not believe in placing the teachings of art or of anything else before children in a way to over-impress and to stupefy. But there is evident wisdom in bringing within the child's intellectual range what it should receive, waiting patiently for development to do the rest. It is painful to think upon the results that one day shall be the outcome of the so-named art-lessons that are daily inflicted upon children. How much they are to suffer from it is evident only after it is too late to mend the evil; how much they lose is an unknown quantity. It is because there is so much in the art-teaching of children that I have laid such stress upon the importance and desirability of teachers becoming specialists in elementary work, for, while it is true that thousands pride themselves on being able to instruct, it is rare that we find one who knows how to begin.   Their methods remind one of a tall man taking a little child to walk suiting neither his speed nor his stride to the weakness of his companion.   He should take the child by the hand, suit his movement to that of the little one, dissipate its weariness by his pleasing words, and, though he does not say it, let him make the child comprehend for itself that its fatigue is the price paid for the great pleasure it has.   Now there is no need whatever of ever changing this relationship; simply multiply it by a few years' experience and the youth is taught in the same way.

I have said previously that one of the best signs of art-progress is the appearance of art-specialists; I have a parallel statement to make here: one of the best signs of progress in art-education is the appearance of art-works for the young.   It is impossible to estimate the good of bringing art and letters within the child's world.   Millet, the French artist, was keenly delighted to study child appreciation by sketching familiar objects for his " little Antoine."   I would recall to you what has been done for the young by some of the most eminent men of our times.   Let me mention a few: First of all there occurs to me the name of Charles Kingsley, whose " Water Babies," " Madame How, and Lady Why" are fascinating to young and old; the name of Hans Christian Andersen is, I hope, dear to all of you no less now than in former days; what Charles and Mary Lamb have done in their "Tales from Shakespeare" has been done by Kingsley about the Greek Heroes and by Alfred Church in his admirable books about Greek and Roman Times; pictures told so beautifully that I wonder more every day why art-educators do not bring these helps into their work. Ruskin's "Sesame and Lilies," "Crown of Wild Olives," and "Ethics of the Dust" must be mentioned. Then there are the "Rollo" books, "Stories from the Arabian Night's Entertainment," and such a host of others that it would be a waste of time to mention them. These books are helpful in their place. I am certainly right when I expect a better lesson from a child whom I send away with one of these volumes to read than I am if it goes away with no definite feeling whatever resulting from my inattentive heed to its work. Children have serious ways which we should enter into with seriousness; they are merry too, and one should know how to share that merriment else he is un-susceptible to one-half, nay more, of the child's nature. But I am not yet done speaking of what has been, and may be, written for children. Of the writers of to-day many pay heed to nothing but the wants of the young; you know what excellent papers and magazines are issued solely for them and a very practical conclusion to draw from it all is this: if such helps are of so much value to the child in the world of its mother tongue, may not similar helps be brought to work in its favor in the art-world? There is only one remarkable feature in this regard, and it is this: the number of art teachers who entertain this thought and carry it out are as one to one thousand. I will not consider in any of these talks the use of trash in teaching, because I regard our opinion on that as one; looking upon you as earnest workers I attribute to you earnest ways. You recognize the value of these juvenile works in music contributed to the child-world by the greatest writers; I will not attempt to name either works or authors. But I will ask, why have you not recognized and employed parallel helps in lines immediately aside from the particular form of key-board that commands your attention? If you are to become ideal teachers of the young in music I should expect you to know what works of each of the great writers, either in the original form or in an excellent adaptation, you may use to advantage to the double purpose of pleasing and instructing. Beyond this I should have you know how you could educate your children in music apart from performance; they should be readers under your wise guidance—and I should require it to be very wise indeed. I should expect that now and then you spend a lesson hour explaining the form and motive-structure of figures that make up the decorative ornamentation of a panel, after which you should take up the music of the lesson and, in parallel terms, explain its form and motive-structure. I am fully prepared for you to receive this suggestion, as well as others I may offer, with the statement that such study is too difficult for children; in reply to which I need only say that if you do not know how to make it not only simple enough for children but luminously clear to them, you are not yet a qualified teacher of the beginnings of art. I would, indeed, like to know that you consider it as much to your purpose to possess, besides music, illustrative means of drawing parallel lessons from other arts. It is not a hard matter for you to gather together admirable photographic reproductions of works of painters and sculptors; of monuments and buildings, of painters and sculptors themselves, of the makers of these buildings and of great authors and composers. I would like you to possess, for example, a volume of photographs of Cathedral architecture, in the Gothic style; it is very easily obtained and should consist of views of the whole edifice and of the most important portions. With the music lesson you give I would have you show your student all

there is to be learned in a moulding; in the tracery
of a window, in the foliation of a capital, in the
clustering of pillars. You should plan for your
student the sonata he might chance to be studying;
let us say the Opus 49, No. 2, of Beethoven. Make
a simple basilica plan, such as one sees in the
parish church of Great Britain. Then show him
the plan of a cathedral, side by side with that of
the symphony. Here the form is larger and
more complex; the original simple parts take on
divisions, which are now thoroughly independent
in one sense and closely knit into a whole in the
other. The parish church was simple in its parts;
the great cathedral has many different parts not
found in its simple prototype; the cloister walk,
the chapter house, the lady chapel, the great east
and west windows, decorated spandrels, the lofty
central tower, the rich coloring—the instrumenta-
tion of the symphony; all these differences would
be great, but they would be comprehended from
the lesson on a simpler type in the beginning.

Without multiplying possible means any further
you are, doubtless, willing to admit that this adjunct to music instruction is admirable but im-
practicable, if not impossible, requiring not only
complex means but a considerable degree of pro-
ficiency in these parallel matters on the part of the
instructor. But you are wrong in your entire

objection. Such educational means are possible, practical, and absolutely necessary *if you teach art as a thing of beauty and of use.* They are useless if you conceive and teach art *as a plaything.* If these suggestions are new to you I would like you to give them practical test, in an earnest way, not in a perfunctory manner. The hints I give you here are meagre enough, but they are enough if you have within yourself the desire to test the value, to the musical educator, of illustrative means drawn from other arts, explained so as to show the independent nature of each, on the one hand, and their close inter-relationship on the other.

I have given you a single instance of this parallel teaching, the other line being architecture, the most admirable side-study that a musician can take up; but there are, as well as it, many others in which you could work with much advantage; the only necessity is that whatever be the nature of the parallel it must be contingent and practical. If you work in the right way you can make it so. To talk with children, or with learners of any age, about what interests them is to instruct them; but it is necessary from the beginning to enlist their sympathies and to teach toward an objective point, using all the practical and beautiful means at your command to help you on. These last four words are the keynote to a very important statement:

any means that helps on education is always a means and is, consequently, secondary to the motive which prompts the use. That use, with you, is to make art truthful and serviceable to all to whom you teach it, and there is no better time than in childhood to lay a foundation for the keen perception and appreciation of use and truth. With years the boy becomes the man, gathering knowledge all the while apart from what he is taught; making it a great and difficult duty to set his mind and keep it to the lathe.

I would have you study the possibilities of a child educated in the constant presence of wise and refined influence. In thinking of this and making observations you will learn that it is a serious matter to misunderstand a child; even more serious to store its mind with educational bric-a-brac that has no meaning. Do not withhold praise for the task well done; the child looks up to you and wants to please; recognize it. That you teach care and method is a foregone conclusion, for nothing that I have suggested here is possible without them. You will be constantly surprised to note how very much children can learn with ease, when they are taught in the proper way, the secret of which is to be a child with the child. You must always meet them in good faith, for children judge intuitively and seldom falsely. You must not forget that the children who study under your guidance are prone to talk about you and their lessons among themselves; you are, to them, an important factor in life; what you give them to do is the subject of their thought, their talk, their dream and their wonder. Interest them in your own work, ask them to help you; it has a good effect upon them, and you would better win their good will in such a simple way as this than lose it by reason of misunderstanding them.

Let me say in closing this talk: not only remember the children as you study the classics in music, but remember them in your library; in all the study you do in music and in other arts; always set aside for them what you know is fitting; a child's thought turned the right way promises a good citizen to the world.

CHAPTER IX.

INDIVIDUALITY IN ART.

A feeling hallowed the spot, as if there yet lingered a low vibration of the lyre, though the minstrel had departed forever.—BAYARD TAYLOR.

If you ever chance to visit the quiet town of Stratford, on the river Avon, you will be surprised to learn, from evidence on every hand, how deep and genuine is the memory of its great son, " our dear Shakespeare," as they are fond of saying. His presence is everywhere, filling the air with its inspiration, causing one's thought now to be retrospective, now to dwell reverentially with all there is in the quiet present that recalls the past. The little town itself is not as beautiful as many another in the Midland counties, nevertheless, there has hung about it for three hundred years the wonderful charm of association. Here Shakespeare was born. That thought seems to hallow the spot. One walks the streets and thinks of him who, unconscious of the tribute the centuries were to pay him, once did the same, revolving in his mind the thoughts that have since been eagerly read by all civilized nations. Or one may wander along the Avon, that flows so quietly by the church where he lies, quietly as if it feared to disturb his slumbers, and one has ever the same thought—of him who likewise wandered here as he wove in magnificent form and color his pictures for the whole world. Then one enters the church and stands by the tomb. How well may one then ponder upon the wonderful influence of a great personality, how powerful it is to draw us to itself, how its teaching, moving ever onward with time, becomes the common property, how it enters into current speech and becomes the household word, how it helps to form our code of moral laws and make us more to one another. To be in the presence of that noble dead makes one a wiser person. No explanation can follow as descriptive of the reverential feeling it creates within, but it is genuine and deep acting. One goes again to the Avon, that twines a few yards from the church door, and finds a moment's rest in watching the gentle flow of that little stream, beautiful of itself and made romantic by the name of Shakespeare.

The most potent charm about any locality is the power of personality; no natural charm excites half so much in him who is a true lover of all that has made to-day as good as it is. The very association of a noble presence makes itself felt all about, and Stratford, and the Bonny Doon, and the streets of Nüremberg are not so much to us in themselves, as they are the stage wherеon Shakespeare and Burns and Albrecht Dürer proved to mankind that they were born to a purpose and lived well up to it. It is this charm that so hallows the old world. Everywhere one finds, power-fully exerting itself, the influence of the past. To the thoughtful mind its inspirational force is remarkable; that is in part why the intellect is so richly stored when it gets its training in an old land; but the mind ere it can gain from this noble past must be finely tuned, else it will not vibrate in sympathy with its rich-toned surroundings; it cannot be synchronous with what is unlike it, for unless the mind is full to overflowing with what it seeks it cannot find it.

After all it is not to be wondered at that we are willing and eager pilgrims to the lands and homes of them whose lives have done much toward making to-day what it is. We turn readily and with eager thought to them because we recognize in what they are and in what they have done exactly what we would ourselves be if we could. The fascinating interest in all biography lies in having displayed before us the means with which personality works and individualizes itself. But after you have cleared away all the novel scene and come to the consideration of the real acting factors in the play before you, it is plainly evident that every man characterizes himself by the way in which he employs his gifts, that his activity is shaped by his surroundings, and that if he works worthily and constantly the place that gave him birth, and where he labored in his ripest years, will ultimately be proud of him, though it may be slow in manifesting this. Men are remembered more for what they are than for what may form the outward events in their daily life. Thus, Philip Melancthon, speaking of his friend Albrecht Dürer, said wisely,— "his art, great as it was, was his least merit." There was in this one more man than artist; if it is not so with every one who would be an artist what can be said of him? It is a pity to keep the gem for years in a mean setting. It is a poor tribute to the memory of a human being, is it not, to say of him after all his years of life, " all he did was to let himself live; he thought nothing of others, did nothing for others, left nothing for others." And it is not alone of you, artists, that one may say this; if the paving-stone is not laid with care the road is bad, if the chisel cuts recklessly into the marble the statue is ruined,—the work has always one value above all others because it is lasting, and that value is determined by *how much man there is put into it.*

I hope you all are keen lovers of biography, and

to this I hope you join one further delight, the study of the people who make your world. In carefully studying out what strength of character and force of surrounding can do you will be led to recognize and to appreciate what is the potency and value of a rare nature. I have chosen this short talk on Individuality because I would have you remember, in your activity as artists, that you are not only developing the self, but that you are adding to the fame of your time and of your fatherland or taking from it, according as you labor. You must not leave an unworthy mark wherever you step; it is as easy to work so that people shall remember with pleasure and grateful acknowledgment that you labored among them. However trifling be the good influence you exert as you go on, it is a possession that brings endless satisfaction and no end of good to others. It is rare, even in centuries, that men live and leave a lasting impression of their being as great as some of which I have spoken; yet no one will deny the truth which says every man's work may be done to the credit of himself, of his home and of his fatherland.

Here are two pictures from the life of Robert Burns; compare them: (1) "This period produced but one poem, his grandest and best, the immortal 'Tam o' Shanter,' a masterpiece of literature, and worthy to rank with anything in Shakespeare or Goethe. It issued complete from his brain in one day, in one magnificent burst of inspiration. He was observed by his wife . . . . to walk hastily along the bank of the Nith, and to mutter as he went. She knew by these signs that he was engaged in composition, and watched him from the window. She afterwards went out to meet him, but he saw her not, and still walked rapidly along 'crooning' to himself. She stepped aside among the broom and bracken to let him pass, which he did with a flushed brow and downcast eye, heedless of the outer world, and wholly absorbed, body and soul, in the transports of composition. No correction was afterward necessary; the poem emerged from his mind complete, without a flaw, inimitable and unsurpassable.

(2) " As he lay on his death-bed, his final hours were embittered by mental anxiety, and by the dread that a hard-hearted tailor, to whom he owed a small sum, would either seize his last blanket from under him, or consign him to the degradation and horrors of a jail. . . . . The little town of Dumfries, the scene of his closing years, and of his death, and which he has rendered classic ground forevermore, did its best to honor his memory. The people of Dumfries knew that he was great and noble while he lived among them, but they

did not know, until they stood sorrow-stricken around his grave, how infinitely more great and noble he was than they had imagined him to be."*

The bed of violets sends out a rich perfume because each single blue-petaled beauty adds a little; nor does one think any the less of them because another single flower is as fragrant as them all. A nation, in the several manifestations of its activity, is typified by the work of single individuals; art, then, in America, is characterized by the combined labor of American artists. In the power of your individuality you exert a considerable influence; you make a place for yourself, you add a stone or two in the art temple of your time, you have the opportunity to stand loyally for any truth that may be made plain to you, you may teach others to build well and you may honor, far beyond any expectation of your own, the journey you are taking. If you do this your past will be bright forever; but it is just as easy sometimes, not to do so; then the past is not bright; so there are two chances, one of which is for you, if you are given to taking chances;—a wise man does not, and what is even better, he need not.

In any kind of work there is a right way to do it. It is not your act in art alone, but in all things, that makes you. Every deviation makes it more

---

* Charles Mackay.

difficult for you, more difficult, too, for others who may trust you as their model. Any work, particularly work in art, demands great self-denial, endless perseverance and ever-increasing knowledge; this is the practice it gives the worker, and this practice makes him an artist only incidentally as it makes him a man.

We are very slow to learn how great a privilege is life. "I have endeavored always," says "Arminius Vambèry, "to be before all a man who, unbiased by any sympathies or antipathies, is anxious to be of use to his fellow creatures without any distinction of race or creed." One thinks that a broad thought to express; it is a far broader thought after one has put it actively in operation. Fortunately the individuality is not formed alone by great events; the smallest exert proportionately as much power as the greatest, and it is easy to lose to sight the fact that even many great events are entirely overbalanced by a multitude of smaller ones.

If, instead of being musicians and students of art, you were all engaged in carving statues, some from small blocks of marble, others from large, would you of the small block endeavor to bring out as great a statue as your neighbor who works on a larger stone? Rather, I think, would each of you try to get the best statue possible with the material you have. Then in the end, when the work is done, people would speak of how you did your task.   Keep that in mind.   " Be we high or low, rich or poor, clever or stupid—for which God cares nothing—it is equally possible for the humblest of us to do our duty."*   The personality is built like a temple, act by act, stone by stone; its solidity is its power.   " It is true I take a long time to paint," said Zeuxis, " but I mean my painting to last a long time."

In the beginning of this talk we spoke of Shakespeare.   Let us do what he has done many a time, walk from his house to the thatch-roof cottage of Anne Hathaway, a mile or so away, in the village of Shottery.   It is a delightful ramble through the fields, just such a walk as one would be fond of taking.   The turf is very green and the clover blossoms very white, as if they try to be as beautiful as they can.   One lingers about the cottage, dwelling reverently with the past, heeding not the present.   As we step out of the pretty garden let us pluck a sprig of boy's-love for it was a boy's love that brought us here.   We go back to Stratford, and above all the town rises the spire of Trinity, stately to heaven.   Then it comes forcibly to us that the lover, and the English girl who walked beside him, across these fields as we are doing, now lie here beneath the distant spire and all the world bends its steps thither in reverence to the noble dead.

* Canon Farrar.

CHAPTER X.

THE BRAIN AND ITS BURDEN.

The cares of life, they say, if carried too far, bring more of pain than pleasure, and war against the health. Thus I praise less what is in extreme than the sentiment of " Nothing in excess," and the wise will agree with me.—EURIPIDES.

The object of all true culture is to aid the designs of nature; and our plans must be carried out conformably to her laws, in order that we may attain satisfactory results.—DR. J. H. TAYLOR.

Take in your hands a violin and pluck its E string; observe its pitch; turn the tuning-pin from you a little and pluck again; the pitch is yet higher; turn a little more and the tone is yet more acute, yet farther and farther away; continue to turn the pin and the tone is ever farther distant; with every moment it is more shrill, more piercing; there are more vibrations and they are more emotional; once more turn the tuning-pin; Snap! the string has broken. The force was too great.

It is very easy to repair the accident to the violin, because the string is easily replaced by another.

Let us suppose, however, that the string could not be replaced; do you not think the player would guard it with the greatest watchfulness? do you think any care he could give it would be too great or any price he might set on it be too high to represent its worth? No. Within reason it will bear any strain put upon it; it will give forth its tone high or low, soft or loud, in answer to the player's will; but there is a limit to its strength and sonority. With very little experience the player learns to know what this means.

No sedentary worker should be ignorant of his power; he should know how much brain-lifting he can do without injury to himself; he must know how to treat the brain as he would the muscle, impose not too much upon it and when it is weary give it the rest nature craves for it. He will learn that as the muscle is used constantly and with reason it increases muscle-power; so the brain used in the same way will increase in brain-power. The muscle over-exerted cries out in pain for rest, immediately or soon after the exertion, that it may regain its condition of quiet, but it is characteristic of the brain to bear its great burden for a while, at the same time storing away pain for the future. "Every nerve that can thrill with pleasure can also agonize with pain,"* and let me add that no pain is

* Horace Mann.

more excruciating than nerve-pain.   It is becoming more and more a part of our educational system, especially in colleges, to consider physical culture along with mind culture.   The Swede, Peter Henry Ling, who made a special study of mechanical movements as an aid to physical self development, has very truly said that " every just attempt to develop the powers of the human being—mental or corporeal —is properly education," and again, he has said, "every movement is an idea expressed by the body."   As much education may be given to the physical man as to the intellectual ; a training that is devoted wholly to the muscular, and forgets the moral man, produces only a brute ; that which is devoted wholly to the brain and refuses the body sufficient strength to keep the intellect healthy is merely a monument raised on no foundation.

No one who has been a student for long can have failed to observe that the labors of sedentary life are not, in themselves, conducive to even a moderate amount of physical exercise.   It soon becomes evident that if the benefits of physical culture are to be enjoyed they must be sought and availed in channels apart from those in which the student life is lived.   In the life of manual labor there is usually enough, if not, at times, too much, physical activity attending the day's work to provide all needed bodily exercise and at the same time to accomplish the wage-earning.　But it is not so in professional life.　One who has led a retired, sedentary life as a student simply enters another phase of it when he assumes professional duties. He has not left the circle, he has simply turned around in it; he regards life from the same point but in another plane.

The evils of sedentary life cluster about none more collectively than about those studious ones who idealize their calling beyond reason; they pay to it such intense devotion, they labor so faithfully and constantly in its behalf that the self is entirely forgotten, or, at best, is thought of only when it complains; and then, how? ruefully, regretfully that it should interpose its pains between to-day's inspiration and to-morrow's hope.

Let me read you a delightful bit of common-sense: "One day I asked my friend Jones to make an appointment with me.　There were good reasons why we should spend an hour together.　Jones consulted his little book.　There was no day, scarcely any hour in any day, that had not its engagement for the next fortnight.　It was a matter of the most elaborate calculation before a time could be fixed.　One day Jones met one of those intensely busy people—rather a distinguished man in his way—down at Westminster.　He spoke, and very truly, of the multiplicity of his engagements.

'I will give you a bit of advice, my friend,' said he. 'Go to Westminster Pier and take the penny steamer to London Bridge and back.' 'Yes,' he answered, with a sigh, 'there are no doubt plenty of cheap amusements around us, only there is no time for them.' Of course he did not take the penny steamer. Instead of taking penny steamers he got ill and died."

Before proceeding to a closer examination of the phases of sedentary life, one fact must be stated,— it has certainly come to the notice of all of you, and it is this: the labor that, with ease, is accomplished by one, is an overpowering burden to another. Strength of mind and body vary as much as sentiment and ability. Hence any advice or warning that may be offered to brain-workers in general can be accepted and applied only relatively. It cannot be said with absolute definiteness, that, in brain work, all of us shall go "thus far and no farther." The power of one river cannot be determined from that of another. Hence the matter of health must be studied individually; for not even our talents vary more than our power to work.

To the art-student physical health is the capital on which the art-life is founded. It gives him a clear brain, sight and hearing not too easily impaired, a steady hand to guide the brush or produce the tone, strength to conceive and carry out a large work, strength for the activity art now demands, strength to bear the varied activities that make up a day's life, strength to do what one should and resist what one should not. A mere glance at the best known biographies show us that physical affliction has deprived many workers in art and letters of a most valuable power. From Bach, it took sight which in early life he injured by too great strain imposed in music copying ; Prescott, the historian, suffered a similar affliction ; Longfellow was obliged to undergo an operation on the eyes for the removal of an evil brought about by reading in the twilight ; Beethoven suffered the greatest loss to the senses that could befall a musician, deafness, the direct result of carelessness in health matters. I have in mind two literary workers ; one is at the present time almost totally blind from over-use of the eyes in early years ; the other has, for a year or more, suffered the delusion that every one was attempting to poison him ; it was but a short step from that condition to incurable insanity and he took that step not long ago. Who can read the Appendix of Wasielewski's Schumann, contributed by Dr. Richarz, without being overcome with sadness ? The constant " A " ringing in the ears, his asking his own little ones whose children they were, his jump into the Rhine, then the drawing of the dark veil over the final days ; I know of nothing in the whole range of biography so sad, so heart-touching as the fate of Robert Schumann.

Nature furnishes but few geniuses at a time, and they are so intensely individual in the work of their mature years that one may or may not chance to write to them. The genius, as we are wont to call a richly-gifted man who works hard, is the flower of the rarely blooming art-plant ; the plant itself is the army of workers, who, with far less ability than their acknowledged leader has, are in some respects no less unique. It is to them that one feels such a talk as this may be properly addressed ; and given and received in the spirit of friendship that looks out for well being. I consider no one the fit guide or instructor who is not able and willing to give thought to the physical well-being of his students. So many little things in student-life betray the over-worked mind and body that I do not comprehend how an instructor can be oblivious of the real cause of the results before him. I con- sider it just as much a part of a teacher's duty to determine in the personality of a student what he has the strength to do as what he should do in art- work. Not too high value can be placed upon this manifestation of personal interest ; and any instruc- tor who refuses to consider it is but partially quali- fied for the office he assumes. Unless one makes as thorough a study of health as of the profession one assumes, the severe employments of sedentary life will bring about "an undue and disproportionate activity of some parts of the body to the detriment of others." When this is the case, and this disproportionate activity is carried to excess, nature rebels, but first, as a warning; just as she has taught the rattle-snake.

The evil, above all others, against which the art-student must guard is nervous prostration. Nature is extremely kind in her warnings of this approaching malady, and her premonitory symptoms are numerous. A feeling of pressure against the brain at the top and back of the head, buzzing in the ear sometimes accompanied by a snapping sensation, as if something had given way; approaching near-sightedness and a floating before the eyes of a speck or curled figure; that tired feeling of the brain that is produced when trying to recall something, which is not exactly a loss of memory but a want of readiness on its part in response to one's endeavor; insomnia; lack of self-control in exciting moments ; these, and many other warnings, are given by nature before a complete downfall is experienced. Only that wise and well-known precept, "know thyself," can shield one from any of these dangers. Learn by observation in what part of the day you can work best; how much work you can do at one sitting; know what are your weak points, and favor them by building them up with care and judicious employment; know how much sleep you require, and how much rest you need in the day, and if there is any reasonable possibility of getting them, so arrange your work as to have the advantage of these helps. Avoid, altogether, the use of soporifics, sedatives and excitants; do not work too late at night, and do not fail to have some unoccupied time between your evening's work and bed-time. Work done at night is usually done with intense interest; the lights, the quietude of the room, the full forgetfulness of the outer world, all combine to put the mind in a peculiar condition, eager and ready to work and to get deep into it. And the danger arises in taking this highly-wrought interest to the pillow. Early in the day and, if at all at night, early in the evening are the preferable times for mental labor. I have in mind a composer, well-known in both continents, whose custom it is to rise early, breakfast, and work in his studio until noon; he devotes the afternoon, until six o'clock, to teaching, and the evening hours are at his own disposal. One can so accustom one's self to such an arrangement as this that little is lost in the way of inspiration or eagerness to work. Habit, itself, will bring to one both inspiration and desire when work-time comes. One who is thoroughly at home in such a habit as

I have instanced, who knows how to get from it and give to it, who waits for its help and puts trust in it, is, indeed, to be envied. And, on the other hand, no work is so uncertain, so irregularly done, so variable in its yield, and, on the whole, of so little value, as that done haphazard, in any fashion and at any time.

There is much to be said in favor of habit in work if it allows time for sufficient rest. Then, only, is rest to be counted on. Art-students cannot, however, always plan to the hour with the exactness of the university student who knows what lecture he must listen to for a month or a term ahead. It may be desirable, for him, to change the order of things now and then, to give a trifle more time here and less there. All that is necessary is that the general good of the plan be obtained. Sometimes, in the carrying on of a piece of work, a degree of momentum is induced that must see the work to the finish; the thing to be done must be done in one heat or ruined, the race-horse cannot stop midway; he must go round or drop out. When the artist finds his task is so well progressing that the spirit in which he labors will see it to the end he is justified in thrusting his plan for daily work aside and making the lesser duty give way to the greater. As a general rule it will be found true in art-study as in business, that the application of common-sense will solve the problem of many a puzzling situation.

Be willing to yield to-day an hour or so in the favor of health rather than be compelled later on to stop altogether. In the early years injudicious tendencies may so far interrupt an art career that it cannot be continued, and the consequence is a life current is changed and a glowing futurity becomes all at once an impossibility.

If you can accustom yourself to logically planned work you have added years to your life; thereby you will be able to sustain an amount of labor that, to the unpracticed worker, seems impossible; if to your well-arranged labor you can add a vacation-time you have the keeping of your health, as far as brain work is concerned, in your own hands. A peculiarity of art-life, as of educational life in general, is the enforced rest of two or three months in summer. Nothing could be better; even if work is so logically laid out that this vaca-tion is unnecessary for health it is valuable in giving one the opportunity to change the scene, to step out of the rut, to look at self and those about. It need not be a time of idleness, but may be an opportunity to direct activity in another channel, so that you gain thereby rest, profit and pleasure. Imagine the artist dropping his studio work in June and spending his summer months sketching out-of-doors, walking, studying the face of nature and getting close to it; a few weeks only of such days bring pleasant themes for reflection that crop up now and again for years. Let us suppose that to your general musical education you add, as a side study, Gothic architecture (a knowledge of which will contribute to your constructive and conceptive powers in a wonderful degree), could you spend a summer more pleasurably and to greater gain than in, let us say, the cathedral towns of England? I see you walking from town to town, all your traveling necessities in a knapsack that you conveniently carry; and such roads as one finds in England! One walks over them for the mere pleasure of it. Days of this out-of-door life, amid rich rural scenes, in the cathedral close, in the cloister walks, in the choir of the edifice, put the mind and body in tune and give rest to the spirit. And the sleep that follows such a day! refreshing, restful and dreamless; in the morning the mind and body are eager for the day, and at night again, just as eager for the slumber they have earned. Two or three months of such life in a year is of value beyond telling. It is surprising, too, how few avail themselves of this educational rest; but I shall have more to say about this to you in our talk on vacation time.

In concluding this, the tenth of our talks, let me say :—

1. Respect the natural demands of body and brain.

2. Great works in art and literature are generally produced in a mental excitement that must be compensated.

3. The restless night, when you are too tired to sleep and afraid to lie awake, means that there is something wrong with your day; find out what it is and stop it.

4. Do not try to do four years work in three; it is not always the best fruit that ripens quickest.

5. You can do more in six days than in seven; it may take you a long time to find out the truth of this statement.

6. Observe, generally, such rules in your work-day that will give you most work and most rest; let the one proportion the other.

7. Have a well-chosen hobby that will draw you away from your main theme now and then.

8. Do not needlessly encumber your memory; it will last for life only on condition that it be respected.

9. The overworked body is at a disadvantage in illness, because it has not the reserve strength with which to combat disease.

10. Overwork in early years may stunt the brain as it does the body.

8

11. Mental anxiety kills as many adult people as does bodily illness.

Pay heed to the care of the eyes. In this connection I can do no better than place before you the following rules.*

1. A comfortable temperature, and especially let the feet be warm and dry.

2. Good ventilation.

3. Clothing at the neck loose; the same as regards the rest of the body.

4. Posture erect; never read lying down or stooping.

5. Little study before breakfast or directly after a hearty meal; none at all at twilight or late at night.

6. Great caution about study after recovery from fevers.

7. Light abundant, but not dazzling.

8. Sun not shining on desk, or on objects in front of the scholar.

9. Light coming from the left hand, or left and rear; under some circumstances from in front.

10. The book held at right angles from the line of sight, or nearly so.

11. Frequent rest by looking up.

12. Distance of book from the eye about fifteen inches.

---

* These rules were formulated by Dr. Lincoln, of Boston. They were published in a recent issue of the *Annals of Hygiene.*

To these let me add another: At the very first indication of trouble with the eyes consult a skilled specialist at once.

Overwork, then, does physical injury quite as often in misdirected endeavor as in too great brain activity. Overwork is not, however, the cause of half the mischief that is charged to it. *Worry* does the harm. With the physical self broken down, may not one ask with fairness: if education be ever so great and remarkable, is it a gain of sufficient value to compensate for a loss of health that can never be repaired? Do not make the string too taut and the tone will always be rich and clear.

CHAPTER XI.

A PARALLEL STUDY IN LIFE AND ART.

Whatever branch of art you may be inclined as a student to follow,—whatever you are to make your bread by, I say, so far as you have time and power, make yourself, first, a noble and accomplished artist; understand at least what noble and accomplished art is, and then you will be able to apply your knowledge to all service whatsoever.—JOHN RUSKIN.

It is my desire to proceed slowly with this talk; not because I think I have ability to make it remarkably interesting over all the others but because we are to learn in it a lesson of value. We are to talk this time of the use and worth of music as a factor in life. *Use and worth*, these are the characteristics we shall seek in it. Before we begin, let me ask, how many of you, musicians that you are, have thought to the utmost of your power, what music is, and what you accomplish or hope to accomplish in living the music-life? This would seem to be one of our first and most constant thoughts; as a matter of fact you will be astonished to learn that this line of inquiry is seldom undertaken, why, I leave you to judge, later on. Let us formulate our inquiries in the following pertinent way :—

1. Is music strong beyond its power to please as a mere amusement?

2. What is there of absolute use in music?

3. What amount and force of truth may be put into music and what taken from it?

4. Why should the quality of thought induced by music vary from high to low?

5. What has taken place in one who, possessing talent for art has had that talent developed by education?

6. What is the mental difference between an educated musician who is in every sense true to his office and one whose sense for art, especially the art of tone, is ordinary and untrained, or altogether wanting?

These queries form the main lines of thought leading to the result we desire. I shall not, however, take them up, one by one, and inquire into them, but I will ask you to listen patiently to what may seem, at first, a long story away from the theme; let me gain your good will in the beginning by assuring you that this is not so. We shall chance upon many interesting discoveries which shall make it clear to you that music is not only a beautiful art but a serviceable one. The love and good faith with which you undertake the study of it are, in themselves, sufficient proof that thought of the highest order possible in you may be the parent of music and may be taken from it. The most common form of thought is speech-thought. We shall, undoubtedly, understand music-thought the better by placing it, for parallelism and comparison, beside speech-thought.

The most primitive tribes of men possess, at first, only a sufficient number of sounds to make known their wants. This very rude language is simply a type of the rudeness of the individual who employs it. His means for action, in everything, will be as rude as this. So long as his language is absolutely nothing else than a prime necessity, his mind is unable to conceive of anything else outside the domain of the necessary; hence his implements for war, for agriculture and for home-building, his manner of employing them, of clothing himself and of eating are not superior in any sense to the plane of his language, which is want, necessity. This condition is the result of man's early warfare with what he at first regards as the enemy-forces of nature. But as he conquers them, he finds that these forces of nature are friendly; having subdued them he begins to study their worth. When he does this his observation is busy, and in a little while we find him paying heed to the plainest manifestations of beauty in nature; the finer, deeper beauties he cannot grasp as yet. Now, the moment man begins to conceive beauty he adopts it—a statement just as true of every one of us to-day, in the phases through which we pass, as of the most primitive savage. We next want to know how he adopts it, and the answer is, just as we do in our proportionate position. His first tendency is to imitate by the work of his hands and mind the little beauty he perceives. His language becomes rudely picturesque. Let me read to you, just here, a few lines from the first lecture of Hugh Blair, on Rhetoric, a book all of you should own: "Accordingly we find, that in almost every nation, as soon as language had extended itself beyond that scanty communication which was requisite for the supply of men's necessities, the improvement of discourse began to attract regard. In the language even of rude uncultivated tribes, we can trace some attention to the grace and force of those expressions which they used, when they sought to persuade or to affect. They were early sensible of a beauty in discourse, and endeavored to give it certain decorations, which experience had taught them it was capable of receiving, long before the study of those decorations was formed into a regular art." Since it is true that in whatever plane man works he is proportionately the same as in another plane, his perception and application of the first principles of beauty in one channel, are simply indicative that he will apply them in other channels. Consequently we find that coincidently with his rude attempt to beautify his speech comes the desire to beautify the work of his hands. He adorns his possessions. His flint arrow-head becomes smoother and more shapely; his arrow-shaft and bow are rudely painted. He marks a site not merely by a rough stone but by a stone with a mark upon it which means something to him and to all of his mind; if it be a heap of stones they are not so much in confusion but are arranged in form, Stonehenge, for example.

In a way parallel with all this he makes other changes until all the man is equal to all he understands. He can now coin a word and can give names, which are generally suggested in nature; that is why we generally find the place-names of savage people full of suggestiveness, and they are invariably poetical. Gradually increasing the circle of his observation, his world of speech grows larger; still he elaborates this daily, and in proportion as he elaborates his speech so he elaborates everything else. Do not fail to remember, as we form this picture, that man can recognize and make something of this beauty only in proportion as he conquers want.

I wish now to take you back a little way. Man's desire to give expression to what is within him takes two forms—sign and sound. He finds that sign cannot be developed as can sound, so he turns his greatest attention to sound. In like manner his sound-language has two forms of meaning: First the sound that conveys to one who hears it the mind-picture of him who emits it ; this in time becomes agreed upon as a symbol for some particular object or sentiment—it is a *word*. Secondly, we have the sound that seems to man to be the only satisfactory utterance of his feelings in the expression of emotion—*not of object*. This is less communicative than word because it is deeper in man ; it expresses what he cannot say in word. He has not merely the power to express want but emotion as well ; both exist naturally in him from the beginning, *only necessity drives the word-language to the front and keeps it there.*

Out of the nature that leads man to express his feelings in sound comes a delight, nay, a power that cannot be escaped, which makes man vary his tones ; they are loud and soft, high and low, fast and slow. He employs every degree of speed, force and quality ; as much in the sounds expressive of sentiment as in words. Together with this inborn love and meaning of tone man has one other gift,— the gift of rhythm. The dances and processions of all savage tribes are rhythmic. The fascination of the motion lies in the rhythm. If you will notice, you will see that little children are in a moment interested by a regular movement,— the swinging of a bright toy, the spinning of a top. So much has this natural tendency for regular motion impressed man that it has been said,—every man is rhythmic. We need not trace this. It is sufficient to our purpose to know that in his development man soon learns to add to the tones expressive of his inner feeling this rhythm that is equally natural to him. Why? Because it is a guide, a measure, a sense to his emotion. How does he get this rhythm? By clapping the hands, then beating with them, stamping with the feet, by striking one object against another. By chance he finds that to strike a hollow body—a gourd, for example— yields a better tone than a solid body—a rock, for example; so he beats the hollow body until it occurs to him to cover its opening with a skin, and to beat that. Then he has found the seed of every form of percussion instrument. Later he stretches a bit of cartilage and plucking it listens to the tone it emits; then has he also planted the seed of every stringed instrument. Now the beginnings of all musical development are in his hands, namely,—song, instruments of percussion, and instruments of the string. There is only one factor needed to make the most of them; that factor is working with them to-day. It is Time.

I have said that man varies his tones. When he does that apart from his material wants *he sings*. And when he adds rhythm to these varying tones, *he sings a melody*. He directs this to God, who gave him the desire and power so to express his deepest feeling.

I have taken you a long way—perhaps an unnecessarily long way—to put before you a picture showing whence man receives the gift of music, why and in what circumstances he most naturally uses it. At the same time I hope you have learned incidentally the nature of music, and its absolute necessity side by side with language, but also its superiority to language as a medium for expressing phases of feeling that baffle word description. In other words: music is the most subtle form of speech. The speech of word and the speech of song existed in man from the beginning. Stern necessity drove the speech in words to the front, but while he learned to talk to others he was learning to sing to himself. He said in words what he needed to say to others, he said in song what he wanted to say to himself, *or to that force within himself which he did not understand.* He thus confessed a higher power than his own or any in nature as he knew it about him. Let me say again, to repeat will do no harm :—

Music is the most subtle form of man's gift of

speech.   He expresses in it what he cannot express in words.

Here is a good point to pause for a conclusion, drawn from what has gone before :—

Music is in no sense mere sensual gratification. It is independent thought of the highest order.

Place that statement of fact beside the popular conception of music, and you will be startled.

You can readily conceive the difference between man's first rude attempt at language and a language of highly developed nature; the result of ages of observation, thought, error and conclusion. Between the first desire to sing and a highly developed musical system there is exactly the same difference.   This shows you the truth of my statement made in the opening of this talk; that man is always the same proportionately—only the plane changes.   In both lines of development we have the same original factors but their power is greater. Every thought in music preserves the two prime qualities we found to be inherent in man's nature; rhythm and varying tone.   Without these there is no music.

Perhaps it would be best if I left you to think out for yourselves what extent of character and of meaning music may have; what character and extent any of the fine arts have. You will readily acknowledge, I know, that no fine art exists to be the toy of whoever may wish to play with it; that those who do so toy with it, act as the child that plays with fire; you will learn why music is so commonly loved.   Taken all the world over, in every age and every clime, there is no art so much loved for itself as music.   I cannot offer you any proof of this statement, but I believe the most extended research would substantiate it.   You will understand now what has been said by one of the best art-thinkers of our time: " It is impossible to direct fine art to an immoral end, except by giving it characters unconnected with its fineness or by addressing it to persons who cannot perceive it to be fine."   One may explain the presence of an evident lack of thought or of liking for music in this: that those who are so constituted naturally, are simply deaf mutes in that form of speech.

We will now go back to the inquiries with which we began this talk :—

1. Is music strong beyond its power to please as a mere amusement?

The question has somewhat of the ludicrous about it after we have traced music from its origin and learned the true desire of man for expressing himself in tone.   We do not find the question any more difficult to meet because music is so commonly learned as a frill,—a fashionable adjunct to an education,—it strengthens the belief in the fundamental reason. Music is not simply the work of the fingers, but of the hand, the head, and the heart.

2. What is there of absolute use in music?

Being one-half of man's speech or the whole of man's deeper emotional speech it, at once, assumes in his life a first place, if he wants it. If he gives it no attention it has no force, but that is the fault of the man not of music. Born, as it is, of the best thought, it raises the thought-plane and there begins a refining influence in the whole being. Hence it is not merely to amuse boys and girls, but to elevate morally and intellectually all people, who are not what I have been led to call musical deaf-mutes.

3. What amount and force of truth may be put into music, and what taken from it?

When an artistic nature undertakes to express itself it gives thought a definite direction and weeds thought as it comes to the surface, so that only the best there is at the moment of expressing it is given utterance. Consequently there is re-flected in the art work only the very best of the writer at the time he expressed himself, and let us not forget in this connection the ebb and flow of the nature within. And, also, let us not forget that of the thousands and thousands of works published to-day but very few are anything more than imitations, and some of them of the vilest stamp; so the art-works produced even in busy "to-day" are comparatively few. It is, indeed, very true that art serves us little if we do not put more than art into it.

4. Why should the quality of thought induced by music vary from high to low?

Because it reflects truly what is put into it. This short answer should suffice, yet I may add that music can never suggest thought as low as language does, and it can surpass it in the other direction.

5. What has taken place in one,—who, possessing talent for art, has had that talent developed by education?

There is more man there, unless this development has been bought at the price of all other. In this case he may be lifted out of sympathy with mankind, which is a serious loss to an artist. Of itself, art cannot unfit a man for the world of every-day, on the general principle that he who works in gold becomes a careful, economizing worker in iron.

6. This last query has been so thoroughly forced into a corner that it has, now, no reason for being, though in the beginning it served very well as a hint to your thought.

I hope you will regard the whole chapter in like

manner, and let it be a hint to turn your thought more fully toward the broad extent of this theme which we have treated but briefly. Still I feel certain that enough has been touched upon to show you that art may be so studied that one shall apply its teaching in all things. If it does not do this for those who study it, they are not gaining all they might from it. Art "gives Form to knowledge and Grace to utility;" the whole truth could not be better expressed. When art fits in life like an ornament on a mantel it has become a mummy. Art is not the balance struck between the worth and worthlessness of its followers but it is the very best thought of its very best guardians.

In bringing this talk to a close I will read you a few lines from the pen of him whose thought began it. No artist can do more than what he bids and not one should do less: "All that I ask of you is to have a fixed purpose of some kind for your country and yourselves; no matter how restricted, so that it be fixed and unselfish." *

---

* John Ruskin.

CHAPTER XII.

THE RELIGION OF ART.

In his essay on Ralph Waldo Emerson, Herman Grimm says: "Men drive through the sciences as we rush through Europe in an express-train. The desired goal is reached, the journey is behind us, but we have had no active share in it, have heard nothing, seen nothing, only paid for our tickets, and passed the time in dreams." It is thus we rush through the arts, to-day, here in America, where we make so much of being ahead of all others in our activity. But we must not forget that, while motion lends wings in some affairs of life, only quietude gives progress in others. In the history of every nation that stands out, sharply defined, in the past, down to remotest antiquity, you will find that the people showed the same traits of character in all they did; and further you will find how true it is that nations are made by the very land in which they live. One of the strongest factors that entered into the character-formation of the Egyptians was their great river—the Nile. It forced from them the scientific knowledge of how to manage this mighty stream for their wants and preservation. The artificial lake, the canal, the Nilometer were actually forced upon them by their surroundings. Living in a land where nature has made everything on the prodigious scale, they learned to think in large forms. On the one side stretches the ocean, on the other lies the desert; about them skirt the Lybyan Mountains, and through the heart of their land runs the river that has been as a father to them. The constant observation of these great works of nature, together with the peculiar religious life of the Egyptians, made it as natural for them to construct an enormous sphinx or pyramid as it was, later, for the game-loving Greeks to become the foremost sculptors of the human form. These nations, like all others that have left to us a distinct history, show conclusively that natural surrounding is one of the most potent factors in character-formation, and that this character-formation is not merely a light reflection, but a deep reality, which shines out of everything to which they put their hands. With every nation the natural history of the land, the religious and domestic life, are three controlling factors in all it performs.

Because it is difficult to show the day to the day, we lose sight of this truth in our own doings; but just as the factors of which we have been speaking were the controlling weights in the balance of national history, so these same factors are the controlling weights in our own national progress. Time and the teachings of the past may modify the influence, but it only can be to a slight degree. Thus you may look in the art of any people for the reflection of their daily life; what forms the staple of thought here shows deep traces of its power there. And art has always flourished best with those who love it best; every nation that has become known for its production of thought-works has become known because it has recognized art and letters as having claim upon the attention of itself as a nation and upon its people as individuals. They have recognized that in the national life they lead as a civilized people there are niches devoted to art and letters in which it is as treason to put any other statue, and all nations that have contributed to the welfare and learning of the modern world have not refused to place these statues where they belong. I have said all this to you that you might better understand what I mean when I say: no nation can simply tolerate art and thereby become an artistic nation. Art must be a part of its life and not a plaything. Julius

Cæsar was philosopher enough to record in his Commentaries that the Belgians were the best warriors among the Gauls, because they were farthest away from all that could detract from their skill and power in warfare. The secret of their power was skill by practice and favorable situaticn. Parallel with this, it is true that the nation's art is a heritage from its constant skill, heightened by the emulation which it takes care to kindle. Art is not an accident.

I have spoken of national-art because it finds a place in the life of a people just as it does in the life of an individual. Each of you will find in your personal experience that simply the truth and nothing else stares at you from the statements I am about to make :—

(*a*) You cannot become artists simply by tolerating art.

(*b*) You will become an artist or a tradesman according as you accept art for itself or for whatever gain you may knock out of it.

(*c*) In your personal endeavor as an artist you contribute good or ill to the welfare of your whole nation according as you conceive art to be an inlet for gain, or an outlet for the best thought you can possibly control.

(*d*) A lack of common-sense goes very ill with pretensions to superior culture.

(*e*) In proportion to your strength of character, you will find in your work an outlet for all you can do.

Let us now talk about these matters. I have purposely chosen the title of this talk because I conceive that if you do not bring art into the relation of the best thing in your life for the outlet of all you are, you will be from the very beginning a failure in the spirit of all you do. Your execution may be wonderful, you may write just as many works for the popularity of your public as you can, but if you do not work beyond the mere effort of your technic or the pleasure and gain of your popular writing, you may win one kind of success, and with it one of the most killing of fail- ures; the former will keep you alive for a time, the latter will kill you forever. Art, to make a deep impress upon the character must be constantly before it for all it is worth *as art*. As I have said in a former talk, art must not be a frill. What is there in a work of art that makes it live? Truth. That is why people of finely-trained per- ception love to linger in the presence of great paintings, to hear great music, to study the spirit of great books.

I have twice spoken to you in a way that threw true art-practice and gain in opposing lights. I do not mean thereby to impress it upon you that art-life is incompatible with the necessity of earning. There need be no antagonism between art and bread-winning. Destruction follows only when art is turned *to no other end than the money it may bring.* But any of you who depend upon art for your living, should live from it without defiling it; it is necessary that you know the difference between sufficient and enough; that you comprehend art as not merely a recreative amusement, and that whatever falls to your hands to do receives your stamp, however you do it.

You all are true readers, I doubt not, far enough, at least, to know that poetry and prose may contain as much truth and nobility as human nature possesses; you know that in this medium of expression— language—there may be as much truth and depth of meaning reflected as man has within him. Since, then, art is only another form of expression, another language whose character and words are strange only to those who never say much in them, there may be just as much truth expressed in it as in word-language, and no power of the artist is too great to make the expression of his message too simple. If you will study the history of art in its influence on men as individuals and as nations you will be glad to learn that every true work of art was created for a purpose. This element of use in art is deeply impressed upon one who spends a little time among the Greek sculpture, for example. Further than this, all works of art, of value as art, display in every feature the sterling common-sense of the maker. I speak now only of works that claim to live beyond a day; if they are not conceived and brought forth in the motherhood of artistic common-sense they must be short-lived. Why should the crop be large if there is rot in the potato?* "So sure as you find any man endowed with a keen and separate faculty of representing natural fact, so surely you will find that man gentle and upright, full of nobleness and breadth of thought."†

I would have you very watchful of all phases of the art-life; you may study them out with advantage. To have been an artist for even a short time already you should know how self-development may come in art-practice; how simplicity of aim and intensity of purpose may combine to aid, each the other; you should know why it is, as we so commonly say, that there is no end to learning; learn the intimate relationships existing between art, science and literature; each is but a mode of thought expression; three idioms for one statement. Thus to get close to the very heart of your daily art-work will not stun you with art's immensity but will

---

* Emerson has, somewhere, said this.
† John Ruskin.

teach you that, little as your individual power may be, it is not too little ; the world must have it, and prizes it most because, being the best you can do, it is what you make it. The religion of art is a strenuous defense of the truth beautifully expressed. Truth, so expressed is art. To paint, compose or study as you ought is to undertake labor that will bring you no public notice for a long time, perhaps never. The principle of Fine Art is always the same ; " there is but one right way of doing anything required of an artist," and that is the artistic way of showing truth to the best advantage. " No man can be more than one thing thoroughly, and I hate half-measures," says Von Weber, and this expression of his, " half-measures," is a very good one. It does not mean that you have failed to become one thing thoroughly because you have reached only half the eminence of somebody else, but because you have become only half of what there is in you,—he means that you are letting too much of your skill lie idle ; he hears you complain of the limitation of your power and knowledge, knowing that if you would use all you have of the one you would gain twice as much more of the other; that is the " half-measure " he hates ; and let me say in full earnestness to you all that nine-tenths of your complaints spring not only from just such " half-measures " but from " quarter-measures " and yet smaller. You talk about building but you do not build loftily ; you talk about building but you do not build to last ; you talk about building but you do not know why you build at all. This use of the fulness of power and the wise choice of its direction is the foundation of religion in art. You possess, rightly, a talent for art only when you learn to make it a truthful and instructive heritage for others.

[I have not said these words to you with the purpose of presenting what is merely pleasing to hear. It would be thoroughly wrong to represent art-life to you in impossible phases by the mere weaving of plausible statements concerning it. It is my hope, and has been from the first, to say nothing in these talks that is not absolutely truthful in every application you can make of it, not alone in the music-life but in the art-life and beyond. No amount of studious acquirement can do much for you unless your motive for action is deeper than the mere fancy to possess that acquirement. Unless, in your work, you appeal directly to the common-sense and common probity of mankind your labor is misdirected. Do not, either through haste or blindness, commit artistic suicide.]

"I almost feel like deploring all fame when I see the fools that worship it," says the poet, Edward

Rowland Sill; perhaps the best and surest way to escape remembrance is to run mad after this very thing—fame, that means anything, even popularity, that sucks every class of being into its wake except him who is too wise to pursue it. The Religion of Art then is simply to pay to it, as your daily labor, as much of honor as you conceive is possible; to set as great store by its well-being and preservation as you set by your own life and happiness; to leave the field of your activity richer for the labor you have done in it, and to do your labor not tolerably but nobly. And thus the Religion of Art is the religion of life, of a day or of the moment you are living.

CHAPTER XIII.

GETTING INTO PRINT.

Where a neat rivulet of text shall meander through a meadow of margin.
—School for Scandal.

I have promised you in each of these talks one leading thought that should be a helpful, serviceable aid; you shall not be disappointed in this one. Having considered our theme as we may think sufficient, I shall leave it to you to draw your own conclusions. For my own part, I mean to paint the picture; you shall hang it as you think best; thereby proving how much or little of artistic taste you possess.

Both the publication of literary and musical works shall engage our attention. We will endeavor to discover what the motives are that make so many men and women, of all degrees of intellectual strength, rush into the publicity of print. Having carried this line of inquiry as far as we may deem it necessary, we shall find reasons in what seems guided by no reason whatever; and we shall be the better able rightly to explain them.

Never before in the history of publication have

139

so many and so varied works been issued. The
tendency is undoubtedly towards an increase; the
cause whereof is worth a study. In England the
number of new books issued in 1890 was 4414,
and of new editions 1321, making a total of 5735.
This does not reach the number recorded in 1889,
which was 6067. Novels, tales, and other works
of fiction numbered 831; educational, classical, and
philological, 615; theology, sermons, etc., 555;
juvenile works and tales, 443; year-books and
serials in volumes, 318; history, biography, etc.,
294. In the first three months of 1891 a prominent
literary journal, published in New York, reports to
have reviewed 128 new American and English
books, announced 491 new books " without comment," and indexed 1914 magazine articles contained in over 250 of the leading American and
foreign periodicals. In addition to this it has
chronicled the publication of 114 French books,
giving lengthy reviews of nine of these, 97 German,
23 Spanish, and 102 Italian books. These last
figures may readily be accepted as representing but
a part of the actual publication of the day.

The music publishers of the United States have
issued in the same time no inconsiderable number
of works, to which we must add the musical publications of all European countries; no small item,
let it be remembered. Of all these works some are

rc-issues, but even deducting a generous percentage in the favor of this republication the remainder is an enormous quantity. One asks involuntarily, what becomes of it all? Those who are well-informed on matters of current publication may read the yearly bulletin of our publishers and find that the greatest part of it not only is, but must forever remain, an unknown quantity. Hence one may fairly ask: to what end were these works written, and what chance is there that the best may make a place for themselves?

The faculty of critical judgment helps us a long way in reducing the quantity which we are considering to lower terms, by showing us that much of it is thoroughly useless and unfit for public attention. Even after this large portion is thus readily thrust aside enough remains to make it a significant question, what is the cause of this apparently great activity on the part of our brain-workers? As far as the purely literary worker is concerned it may be stated on the best authority that the best publishing houses in America and Great Britain issue less, by far, than five per cent. of the manuscripts submitted to them by writers. Even the censorship that thus turns away from the public ninety-five or more per cent. of the writing that is doing, does not prevent a considerable amount of valueless work from finding a place in the book-stores and libraries. In music, the amount of trash of the lowest order that succeeds in becoming known to the public is enormous. Every one of you can readily verify this statement. We must not lose from sight, in this inquiry, that the appearance of works of a low order, both in literature and in music, may be accounted for in one way, to a certain extent; there is a public demanding them. But let it be said to the credit of our best publishing houses, that they leave the handling of such goods to those who desire it; so it is not a difficult search in these days to find publishers who bring out only the best works, but it is even easier to find another grade who suffer themselves to print a good or passingly good work now and then, as a reputation-offset to the steady stream of low-class publications that come from their printing rooms. As a general rule it is true that the publications of the day, whether of high or low order, answer to some want in the purchasing public; and further, a very superior work has many more chances of failure than a moderately poor one. In his Essay on Emerson, Herman Grimm says that not for twenty years were five hundred copies of Emerson's "Nature" sold. In the same time many a work patched together for money-getting sprang up and disappeared; and no doubt not a few of them were immensely popular for a brief day.

You know how the publisher greeted Beethoven when he asked what he might hope to receive for his first three Sonatas. It is true to a remarkable degree that what constitutes our classical musical literature was the means of very little money return. The same is true to-day. Even the literary classics have in times past been most ill-paid. Johnson's Rasselas was written in the evenings of a single week for money to pay the expenses of his mother's funeral. Goldsmith received £60 for the " Vicar of Wakefield," Miss Burney received £20 for " Evelina," while for " Cecilia " she received £2000; and yet " Evelina " is undoubtedly better known than its over-paid for predecessor. Dumas received nothing for his first novel, and contributed £12 to the printing of it. He is not alone in that. For "The Lives of the Poets" Johnson received £300. Among the many instances of slight payments for the highest class of literary work are others, however, of the more generous treatment of the author. For " Waverly " Scott received £700. Lord Lytton's works are said to have brought £80,000. The total profits on " Romola " exceeded £10,000. Gibbon gained £10,000 by writing the " Decline and Fall." In all these instances it must be remembered that work done to order has invariably brought larger profits than that done from the pure love of doing. The question arises, which of the two ways of writing is the true way?

In the publication of musical works it is not easy to find many examples of striking financial success. There are some well known to all of us, it is true; and let it be remarked as we go on that few of us would care to be known as the authors of these financially successful works. I do not mean thereby that we are to hold in contempt the author and composer whose works prove a monetary success. I simply mean that the very best of musical compositions do not pay and never have; while on the contrary great sums of money have been made from works of the crudest sort.

In the field of musical literature I fear the aspiring writer will encounter as many difficulties if he wishes to gain a rapid fortune as the young composer. In the arts and sciences literary work falls most reasonably into the hands of the specialist, and there is, you may depend, a thorough weeding out even among these before much money changes hands, so that the chances of the musical literator to increase his fortune are very rapidly reduced to their lowest terms. Even such special work as criticism is often, especially in America, poorly paid. If the critic's income is large you may safely conclude that he is called upon to exercise other faculties as well in the gathering of his funds.

We may now inquire of our would-be author :—

a. Do you publish for money?

b. Do you publish for self-satisfaction?

c. Do you publish because you can do some good with your intellectual wares?

We may, I think, safely conclude concerning the gains of composers, that it is rarely one receives an equivalent for a good work; as a matter of fact it is true that a conscientious writer, true to the dictates of the highest art and unwilling to sell its purity for gain, may not reasonably hope to win considerable money reward by publication. It is equally true that much money is made by writers of crude works lacking every vestige of artistic truth. In other words, in proportion as one will sell out his perception for true art-principles he may make money by musical composition. Take notice that I say he *may* make money. This is an exceedingly unsatisfactory statement to make but it will bear investigation.

That one should so far pander to self as to rush into the publicity of print by whatever means he may command is a direct weakening of dignity. It may mean pleasure to one who sees his name in print, but if he can write only the mediocre, or

10

repeat, in a way that is thoroughly conventional, what some one else has said, he has done good to no one. A writer or composer who has no good whatever to offer the public to whom he appeals has no right to claim their attention. It can only be regarded as a species of dishonesty to claim the time and thought of another by inferior work. If one has not done his utmost and has not a valued vein of thought to offer, there is certainly no reason for availing of publication. The only thought a composer may have concerning the public to which he directs his work is, that by working faithfully, he may succeed to exert a trifling influence for good on the people of his time, and a trifling influence of this nature is the worthiest recompense an author can receive.

Do I mean by all this that I would discourage you as writers? By no means. I would have you write daily; in words and in music. If the thought be properly directed you cannot write too much; all you observe and think and learn may some time have a value for others as for yourself. Guard it until then. Or it may be that only a grain or two of what you gather will have worth. Then save it all for the sake of that grain or two. I would have you constantly observe and ponder. Consider for a moment what a good thought is; a ray of light breaking from a star and that star your soul, given you by your Creator. So I think, and you will agree with me, that to entertain your soul is not a question of your fancy but a duty. Think what rich truth we should have lost if every teacher of times past let thoughts that promised to be good to all, slip away. One may have the most idealistic fancies or the most practical ideas; if they are to be offered in print they must be appropriately prepared. Not the least grain of care should be spared; no labor should be regarded too great that helps shape a thought and so make it serviceable to others. You young composers who think it smacks of vulgarity or of the common-place to copy the same composition four or five times, making it a trifle better each time, will find out one day that you have lost much experience and food for observation and reflection in scorning to study a work sufficiently to see how you may improve it from time to time. Prof. Huxley has more wisdom: " I have learned to spare no labor upon the process of acquiring clear ideas—to think nothing of writing a page four or five times over if nothing less will bring the words which express all that I mean, and nothing more than I mean."

Let us suppose you would be a composer. You determine that the public shall know the vein of your thought; and you will write a song that shall show it. When it is done, let me ask you to step into a music store and look at a score of songs by famed writers, perhaps all of them are known, and your own may be the equal of not one of them. One sees at once your inexperienced thought, and what is more, there is evident your intention; namely, to get into print. You will admit that with this stamp affixed, your song makes but an ill appearance in good company. The amount of this kind of work that may be found in print is enormous; bearing not a vestige of originality, every example shows plainly traces of distortion, of poverty of ideas, and of the imitative principle that is so strong in over-anxious composers, of little thought and less experience. The best art work is undeniably that done for the love of art; even one whose gift of genius is limited may produce most admirable results when guided by this principle. On the other hand I can very well imagine that a composer of much ability and experience can sufficiently command himself to write, let us say, a group of songs, to order, and acquit himself well. I cannot, however, imagine that work, good for anything, can come from one who has little experience as a patient worker but a strong wish to rush into print. I am not drawing for you merely a picture; it is unfortunately an actuality. The number of people who are burning with the anxiety to establish public claim to a very poor musical composition is great enough to raise one's astonishment.

The question may naturally arise in you: Why do music publishers accept works of so little merit? Some do and some do not. It is a pleasure to know there are some who do not. That others do must be explained in two ways: As there is a demand for chromos and very cheap prints, for low class novels and worthless story papers, so there is a demand for almost any concoction of sounds with or without words. By some mistake we call it music, but it is not music. One other reason is this: There has not yet come into music publishing a censorship as severe as that which obtains in the literary market. [I say "market" justly. The moment a musical composition is published the publisher cares very little for the inspiration you may have had; it is to him an article of trade in which he sees money, or he would not handle it.] That the music publishing houses have what is termed a "reader" only means, as yet, that this personage admits too much that is valueless, that he does not refuse enough. Yet, as I have hinted above, a publisher who desires to make money refuses nothing that has money in it; it may be simply poor or it may be simply bad; it is all one to him. It is not difficult to determine his value in art history.

Now, what I would have you conclude from all I have said is this: That you have no need to consider but one question regarding getting into print, and that question is this: Can you by so doing accomplish any good to others? If you can, you are justified in so doing, and it will be expected of you, that whatever you have to say be said in an artistic way, free from affectation, while conveying simply and forcibly the thought you have in mind. The more you are influenced by a desire to glorify yourself, or to add to your fortune, the less, in proportion, will you succeed in accomplishing the good that should be your only motive. An Italian historian has keenly observed, that some of the early architects who have left remarkable monuments to their skill " have not even left us a name on their buildings." If you resolve in the beginning to write only the best you can, and feel that you can offer your work as freely without your name upon it as with, the spirit in which you labor will be good. Determine from the outset of your career that you will eschew all forms of publication which foster nothing but vanity. If they exist for that purpose alone they can do no good, and if they can do no good you should have nothing to do with them. If you would be successful in your choice of a theme for publication, either in musical composition or in a literary way, first determine what is needed that will command your best thought; then endeavor to fulfil the want with credit to yourself as a writer and to the good of those who study you.

As a bit of parting counsel let me say, write your best, put it away that you may forget it; when it has ripened bring it forth for the further improvements your increased knowledge and impartial judgment can add. Do not compose and publish music for money; if you must compose, do so for the love of it; if you must make money, make it some other way. The chances that your composition may be a financial success are few. The better your composition, the less willing the publishers will be to pay you anything for your work, unless you can embody in it an original idea that shall have value in the art-world. There is always value in ideas. Cherish those that come to you, and do not play too many variations on old themes; they are not successfully passed off for new. One of the most widely-known writers of the day has said concerning literary work: " Hardly half a dozen in ten thousand can expect to make a living out of it." In musical composition the chances are so much less that scarcely anything is left. It is equally true in music and the world of letters, that authors are driven from the pure to the impure because the one will not yield a livelihood and the other may. It is best not to write for the living. Composers of music are art-builders, not art-despoilers. Looking at the works published from day to day we must conclude that a great many of our musical writers need more brains, more precision, more mental training and a more worthy object.

CHAPTER XIV.

STYLE IN COMPOSITION.

If a man has anything to say he will manage to say it; if he has nothing to communicate there is no reason why he should have a good style.—GEORGE MacDONALD.

Probably the finest passages have been written without a consciousness that they were fine.—AUBREY DE VERE.

No one strives so much to gain a style in writing as the man of few ideas. Writers who are fertile in richness of thought and depth of meaning impress us, first of all, with what they say; it is only after the meaning has worked upon us that we think of their manner of expressing it. There is only one short definition of this much used word, and that one, of Buffon, which you all have heard many times and which you are now to hear again —Le style c'est l'homme. That sentence contains enough to stand alone for this talk, and it should do so if I thought you would patiently study out all it means; but as, in all probability, you would stop before you had fairly begun, we shall go on and talk about it. Try to find how much a question of personality is style, how it comes not by the seeking but by the broadening of thought in the one who has it. An English writer, Joseph Hatton, has said, " The chief secret of Macaulay's style lies in setting forth in every sentence either a fact or an idea." Now, any form of composition that lacks facts or ideas lacks the very qualities for which the art of composition exists. All forms of expression, whether in language or in art, must carry a thought ; this thought gives value to the work ; a valuable thought rudely expressed has yet all its value, but a beautiful expression of nothing is too evanescent even to give pleasure for more than the passing moment. The foundation of all forms of composition is :—

(*a*) Something to tell.

(*b*) Knowing how to tell it.

In all forms of thought-expression we photograph ourselves ; consequently this " something to tell " will simply be a picture of our strength and form of thought, colored by education, observation and natural tendency. Knowing how to tell it is the manner and force of expression, conditioned by several things ; force of thought and vividness of mind-picture, training in the actual practice of thought-expression, observation and study of the best works in the same and parallel lines of writing, earnestness of thought to be conveyed, and depth of character. All of these enter deeply into any form of writing simply because they enter even more deeply into the individuality of the writer. The painting is but a poor expression of the artist's conception, for if he were not greater than the picture he paints he could not paint it.

You see, even now, that any serious consideration of composition or of any form of writing, starts with thought; thought must be the staple; we see that the scribblers of meaningless verses and inane "pieces" of music, being the authors of no thought, commit a crime against literature and art by giving to the public the poor work which they would have recognized as the worthy. As the chief requirement needed in writing what is worth regarding is thought, so the most striking quality it can have is individuality of character; it is this that is felt, it is this that gives color and value; and it is this individuality of character that so marks composition of any kind as to give it what may properly be called style; for, you will remember, style is the man. Having discovered this, you now know what is wanting in those personalities that are led to perpetrate before the public treasonable acts against pure art and literature.

I hope you will find time some day to study the growth of pure thought-expression in that Danish writer whom I have mentioned to you before, Hans Christian Andersen. In his autobiography, "The Story of My Life," there is a letter addressed to him by Bastholm, the friendly editor of a West Zetland paper. It is worth reading in this connection :—

"I could wish that your juvenile essays were not printed, as I cannot see why the public should be encumbered with imperfections—we have plenty of that; still, they are so far good that they may serve to justify the support you receive from the public. The young poet must shun the infection of vanity, and watch over the purity and strength of his feelings. . . . Observe closely nature, life, and yourself, that you may procure original material for your poetical pictures; make a choice from the things that surround you; reflect from all points of view on what you see; take up the pen, become poet, as if you did not know that any poet had ever existed in the world before you, or as if you had not to learn of anybody; preserve that nobleness of mind, that purity and sublimity of soul, without which the wreath of poetry never can crown a mortal." It is with ideas as with metal in the ore, it must be worked into serviceable shape before its use is fixed. The thought which underlies all valuable expressions must first take form, and thus, too, it happens with children of the mind, they grow as they sleep. The staple of what I may call *ripe* writing is ripe thought. Let the form it takes in the beginning remain until the mind has risen above it, then the acquired skill of the writer will come into play, will change this passage, cut out that, make this part longer, that shorter; and thus, bit by bit, the work becomes more perfect. One must smile at the haste and thoughtlessness of the army of young writers who would put their work on paper to-day and take it to the publisher to-morrow; it is work conceived and executed in a hurry; haste stamps and kills it. Only talented writers of much skill and practice do good work in a short time; and even with them it is probable that their work would be better if done more slowly. You all know the "Elegy"; Gray was eight years in writing it. How many of you know or ever heard of the drama "Die Drusen," written by Johanne von Weissenthurn, in eight days, when she was but twenty-five years of age? I think it is Mary Russell Mitford who says: "I write with extreme slowness and difficulty. I am the slowest writer, I suppose in England, and touch and retouch perpetually." Many of Miss Mitford's stories were written ten or twelve times. Mary Linskill, an English writer of the present time, relates: " an elderly friend told me that Lord

Brougham wrote his celebrated speech on the trial of Queen Caroline, fourteen times."

I have purposely related these instances of how some works have been written that you might deduce for yourselves the second great requirement of the earnest and talented writer—it is painstaking work and plenty of it. I have now some parallel statements to make.

(*a*) The warp and woof of composition are the best thought you can command.

(*b*) The weaving of it is plenty of painstaking labor.

(*c*) The general character of expression in the finished work is style.

(*d*) The power to give the highest polish to the work comes from natural ability and continued practice, well directed.

(*e*) Read the preceding items *a* and *c* and remember what Buffon says: " Le style c'est l'homme."

(*f*) Likewise read items *b* and *d* and remember what Carlyle says: " The grand schoolmaster is practice."

Having learned the full value of these two chief elements of literary or artistic composition, thought and labor, there remain many important subsidiary matters for consideration, as—choice of theme, form, motive of writing, clearness of expression, and general character of the idiom. All of this has been admirably expressed by Rufus Choate. In his diary for 1844 he thus notes the characteristic points of a good speech; they are also those of any work in art or letters: "Truth for the staple, good taste for the form, persuasion to act for the end." Nothing could better typify in few words the leading traits of any art-work. Apply it for yourself either in art, letters, or nature, and you will appreciate how admirable it is in its wide and general application. In selecting themes for expression be led by the natural bent of your genius and character. When wise speakers speak, it is of their earnest thought; they do not pitch blindly upon any theme. You have only to look over the pencillings of amateur writers to find how little guidance they get from thought, and how much they have tried to express what they do not feel, nor have ever felt. Every expression you put into your composition must come from within, otherwise it will not have the stamp of your individuality upon it. Simply to write what you think may please, but what does not carry with it pure thought and style of expression, is surely wasted and wrongly-used endeavor. [Do not mistake my meaning in this. I am speaking of poor writing from those who need not write poorly; not from those who can write no other way.] In the manuscript department of the British Museum one may see a letter written by Browning; it is so full of just what the author in any school of thought-expression should have within him for motive that I will give it place here: "I can have but little doubt but that my writing has been, in the main, too hard for many I should have been pleased to communicate with; but I never designedly tried to puzzle people, as some of my critics have supposed. On the other hand, I never pretended to offer such literature as should be a substitute for a cigar or a game of dominoes to an idle man; so, perhaps, on the whole, I get my deserts and something over—not a crowd, but a few I value more."

We will not speak of Form here; another talk will be wholly upon that theme. Of Motive you cannot have failed to gather enough to make your aim in writing pure, from the two letters I have read to you. "A kingdom of ideas streamed through me," writes Andersen, "and with such a fulness that none of them fixed themselves upon paper." The motive for putting pen to paper is to express this fulness of ideas that so takes possession of one that he is their prisoner. But, in the expression that follows the opening of the flood-gates of thought, if every word, every note, every line cannot be explained and their worth and place defined, the expression is not equal to the thought and the writer must try to make it better. Continued study of the best models in that form of composition which you practice will give you the best help; at the same time you should not fail to study with equal closeness the best compositions in all forms of art. Learn the music of prose and poetry, the beauty of form and color in painting, for all these helps give the musician valued hints. So many authors have a fine sweet air running through everything they write that their worth as exemplars is of untold value to the young writer. Thought that is worth anything is worth addressing to its audience in a clear and open way. Want of clearness in writing means want of clearness in thought, and whoever is not of clear thought should not address his work beyond himself. I can recommend to you, as a little time well-spent, the careful examination of poor works in music, literature and art; as lessons they have value; yet is that sufficient reason for their existence?

Wherever many thoughts are to be brought together and united into a whole like the tiny parts of a mosaic, there must be order, symmetry, form and proportion. You know that a flower is graceful in any position; it is because it combines all these qualities—order, symmetry, form and proportion; it is most beautiful, however, on the plant that bears it, because there it has the advantage of the most favorable situation nature could provide for it. The wisdom of form and situation throughout the plant-world is full of admirable lessons to you, workers in art; I would like to have you read the little essay, "On Leaves," by Sir John Lubbock, so well that you could readily apply its teachings everywhere, most particularly in your own work. Nature is the foremost teacher of the economy of ideas. Ever since man has turned his attention to the ornamental, he has learned and copied her ways.

The best test for the worth of any brain-work is Time. Never hasten your compositions into print. Keep them by you until they are old and well-known to you; they will gain in value by so resting. Now and then we hear of a work being " dashed off;" as an almost invariable circumstance, good works are not dashed off but quietly led forth, and to their author they are old before any one else knows of them. Young artists in every school do poor work for one or both of two reasons, either they commit themselves to public notice too soon, or they do not use the file enough; their work is rough because they do not take the pains to make it smooth. Any composition that is to be known to yourself or to others than yourself as the work of your brains *cannot be done too well.* I have said that when you write you photograph yourself—do not let it be a caricature. When you write do not strive after style, but for the best expression of your meaning; that, you will discover, is style; but it does not come for the seeking; like fame it is simply a result. Not merely surface finish will do in your compositions, they must be finished in every detail. The German sculptor, Rietschl, alluding to the exquisite finish of the Parthenon marbles says: "Every time I call to mind the fact that the backs of the Parthenon statues are as perfectly finished as the front, I am not only filled with wonder and admiration, but deeply touched.* When you stand in admiration before a bit of exquisite cabinet work you do not always think through what changes the wood before you has passed—of the lofty tree whence it came, of the clime in which it grew, of the mosses and insects that lived upon the bark, of the winds and rains that blew about it, of the months, perhaps years that it lay about the workshop until the master workman should pronounce it fit for use. A simple thought may pass through as many stages and find a place at last which it fills so well that one is led to think it was born there.

The material, then, out of which all artistic composition evolves is thought. It must be well trained, highly polished, expressed in a scholarly

---

* A History of Ancient Sculpture. L. M. Mitchell. p. 363.

way, and not forced into a situation that is not fitting to it. The composer must possess not only an artistic nature but this nature must be cultivated by artistic training. The way in which he expresses himself should grow directly out of what he has to say. By much and continued observation among the best works of art he should be learning constantly what means he may enlist to help him gain yet a better manner of giving expression to his mind-picture. So long as he writes he will write better, and the way he writes will grow out of what he has to say; because what he has to say is a part of himself, and he, himself, is the style.

CHAPTER XV.

FORM IN ART COMPOSITION.

One must be able to make use of the trivial for the expression of the sublime.
—Jean François Millet.

Any expression of thought must have shape, or Form ; the clearer and more logical is this Form the more valuable it becomes as an idea. Form assumes its highest importance when it fulfills the mission of presenting most forcibly the thought it clothes. In consequence of this there are two chief outlets for Form-value, namely, Form that aims at Use and Form that aims at Beauty ; out of these spring another, Form that aims, at the same time, at both Use and Beauty. In literature the poetic sense aims at expression which unites Form and Rhythm, to which there may or may not be added, Rhyme. Thus poetry comes, a more beautiful, more shapely expression than is possible in prose. It is the keen recognition of the beautiful and a formful, artistic expression of it, that makes the poet. If you will patiently examine the sequence of thought and the manner in which thought is expressed by the best writers of prose and verse, you will be astonished to learn how much plan of construction underlies their work. Thought is not best expressed in a hap-hazard way, either in art or out of it. A chief fault in much art and literary production that floods the market to-day is the absence of this one principle of formful thought-expression. It has not shape and, as an attendant evil, it has in it no evidence of thought-economy. Many young writers fail, not because they have no thought to express, but because they have no knowledge of how to express it. No writer, and assuredly no student of art, can afford to remain a stranger to the beautiful manner of thought-expression that has always clothed idea in the clearest form, that has given it the best setting. Form develops with the art it perfects, and is itself the most potent factor in the development.

The application of Form in music as a means of heightening the value of the idea is always extensive; always clearer and more potent as the art has advanced, and always most pronounced in the works of the best writers. This is only one of the many possessions common to music and much else in art and nature. A knowledge of its principles is invaluable to the conception of any work of value; without it interpretation loses one most powerful factor. It is perfectly just to say to you that there are not enough art-students who study the synthesis and analysis of music, and further than this, enough of you do not study these two very important matters elsewhere than in music. I shall speak freely to you, in this talk, of the general adaptability and varying manifestations of Form as it may be studied by any of you, in the hope that by so doing you will be led to study Form in music by earnest observation of Form out of music. In no other way can you become keen and accurate judges of the value a work of art may receive in its plan of construction. Always keep it in mind that Form in music means that music is susceptible with many other things to the influence of Form; hence Form is more than it seems in music, for this is merely one of the many channels in which it finds expression.

Everything in art should have a meaning ; otherwise the expression has not been carefully considered. Ruskin has taken pains to say a warning word to students of art, regarding this : " Whenever you take a pen in your hand, if you cannot count every line you lay with it, and say why you made it so long and no longer, and why you drew it in that direction and no other, your work is bad." It is on this principle of every line, dot, note and word meaning something that thought comes to have value. That Form in art is not artificial means adopted by common consent and tolerated simply for its usefulness, I shall now show you, expecting, however, that you will verify the lesson for yourselves by repeated observation and careful thought bestowed upon what you discover; without this whatever you learn will pass by quickly and leave no impression.

In nature Form is a predominating law; one finds its beautifying effect in leaf, flower, fruit, snow-flake, frost, all forms of crystallization, in seeds, like the acorn, chestnut burr, head of wheat, winged seed of the maple, plantain stalk and fern frond. In plant-life order and symmetry obey laws that are most fascinating to study. You all know the Coleus; note how symmetrical and well-balanced are the last leaves, forming, especially in the last four pairs, a cruciform figure of exceptional beauty which is heightened by brilliant coloring. Many plants having opposite leaves in alternate pairs present this same cruciform figure, and one very readily sees whence came the idea of designing the diaper-pattern work which represents a cross of four leaves with a bud in the centre, a figure especially employed as a decorative feature in Gothic architecture. It would be a good hint to bid you note what plants present this leaf arrangement; you can study it in the Coleus, Hydrangea, in the last four leaves of the Gloxinia, and in many others which you would do well to discover for yourself. A similar figure much used in decorative art is suggested by the petals surrounding a berry-like group of stamens and pistils such as one finds in the Cherry-blossom, Cinqfoil, Buttercup, Hyacinth and Barberry. The leaf has been constantly employed in decorative art; frequently in the Norman (Gothic) Capital, in the Corinthian Capital of the Greek Architecture, in the Composite Capital of the Roman, in Gothic Diaper Work, in panels, spandrels and screens. One is astonished at the rich decorative means attainable from so simple a pair of motives as the oak leaf and acorn. In the Cathedrals of Europe one can study this use of motive in decorative art to excellent advantage; you should certainly make it a part of whatever European study you undertake. In America there are good opportunities open to students to study this work in the few excellent museums of our cities; reproductions of baptisteries, panels, altar-decorations, mouldings, brackets, capitals and frieze ornaments are to be recommended for study; the value and meaning of the figure as a whole is first to be considered, then its larger divisions, then its details, the number of its motives, their value employed alone and in conjunction with others, and let me advise you never to lose from sight the economy of thought displayed in the work; it is one of the greatest tests of a fine artist.

Always in decorative art one finds symmetry in arrangement and numerical order in parts. Just as nature constructs the flower in parts of three or four or five, so the artist has learned to be consistent in the simple numerical form that he adopts as an ornament; this, with balance of the main divisions, gives a pronounced character of construction that is beautiful in itself, and the very best exponent of the beauty it is the means of representing. The yellow Oxalis illustrates, in its blossom, the unity of numerical arrangement so clearly that I will have you look at it. First of all there strikes you, the brilliant petals, five in number; back of them the slender sepals, also five in number; but one must look deep down within the flower to see to advantage the full beauty of this consistent arrangement. Foremost is a row of stamens covered with reddish brown pollen that is in beautiful contrast with the delicate tint of the petals and of the same number; beneath these five stamens are five others, and below these latter, one sees the circle of pistils, of whitish green, seeming modestly to retreat within the flower; there are five of these pistils, they being the fifth circle of five parts that we observe in the flower. Of this plant the flower is the most beautiful part; its obcordate leaf is, in itself, of symmetrical shape, but there is no law of number that rules how many or how few leaves shall spring from the root-stalk, or how many flowers shall spring on the flower-stalk. Beginning with leaves and flowers in mass, noting the form on the whole, then moving to the study of parts, one is delighted at the beauty of form and feature which I have outlined concerning the flower. A little observation will make one keen to detect nature's law, and I can assure you the study of it is ever amply repaid. There is an interesting fern, known to the botanists as the Davallia; varieties of it are common in our green-houses; select of this plant two fronds of the same shape and size, place them end to end, and you will have one of the first principles of decorative art illustrated in a way that will impress you. Then study your fern frond and note how the entire form is repeated to minute portions, just as the tree is repeated in the larger limbs, then in the branches, then in the subdivision of the branch, and lastly in the twig. Thus speaking to you of this fern makes me think to say that nature usually gives much grace and symmetry of form to plants that do not blossom; lift a long spray of English ivy and, holding it between yourself and the light, look at the *back* of the leaves, noting their individual shape and arrangement along the stem. As you arranged the fern fronds you may also place end to end four leaves of the Primula * in cruciform arrangement, leaving space enough in the centre to place a single blossom, and in that arrangement note how full of value is the pentagon in the centre of the petals. Once you begin to put these homely hints in practice you will find no end of the possible studies in form one may make in nature's domain; nothing is more delightful and nothing furnishes a better key to the explanation of the use, selection, and arrangement of motives in all branches of decorative art. One need not wander far on this path of investigation to discover the truth in what Millet once said to a student of painting: " The man who finds any phase or effect in nature not beautiful, the lack is in his own heart."

Turning from the works of nature, where we find form in its pure expression, to works of man, we see that in objects of use or beauty Form is a predominating feature. Frequently fifty per cent. of the diamond is lost before its form is secured. In the cutting and setting of precious stones one may see the important rôle that symmetry of form and arrangement plays in securing a beautiful gem, sensitive in every turn, to the light. In every department of the architect's work form is a leading

---

* Primula Sinensis.

feature that aims to be a service and a use. All objects of use in daily life are more or less ornamented by symmetry of form beyond what the actual use demands, which proves that form in art is merely a more highly developed expression of form that exists in nature and in almost all departments of the world of use. But everywhere that form exists you will find beneath it an idea, and through the form this idea is better expressed; the form itself, however, *without the idea* has no value. It is form without idea that produces the rhyme with no sense in it; the artful conversation with no thought in it; it is form without value that imitates the precious stone in cheap material, and so on through a longer line of instances than would be of any value here.

In music, form is a most potent factor toward heightening the force and beauty of a work. Unity and contrast may be found quite as strongly applied in the smallest song forms as in the largest movements of the higher forms. No study in music offers more of real interest and value than the careful study of form, and I recommend it to be brought before students from the first. At the same time that you begin this study you may also begin the elementary study of the ornamentation applied to decorative art; thereby gaining a knowledge of form as a feature in all the arts and not merely a shadowy idea of its application in music alone. The individuality of each of the fine arts demands a certain application of the principles of form peculiar to itself but, like many flowers, apparently different, that belong to the same family, so all these applications of form are reduced to one general principle and are to be regarded from one point of view. Even in music one can find a wonderful change in form use as practiced in the different periods of musical history. It begins in unclearness, grows remarkably vivid and well-defined up to the present, and promises to be strongly influenced by the developments of romanticism. The earliest harpsichord and clavier pieces seem to have been written in the dark, yet in their historical position they are remarkable examples. In the Suites of Bach and Händel, form is simply the bud that bursts into a beautiful flower in the writings of Haydn, Mozart, and Beethoven. The Romanticists retain the same charm of form, give it brilliant coloring, and increase the richness of ornamentation, especially in the profuse use of small groups which serve as decorative motives.

A pure application of form in classical writing is found in the works of Mozart; a volume of his sonatas is a full treatise of form as applied to classical music. Standing between the Contrapuntal and Romantic Schools, what Mozart writes readily explains what has gone before and furnishes a key to all one finds in Beethoven, who is, in turn, the initiator of early Romanticism. Everywhere in Mozart there are found most beautiful means employed to heighten expression and force. And always the simplest means does the most. Even a hasty observer will notice how fond he is of certain motives, especially this group, which is to be found innumerable times in the Sonatas alone. Careful observation will teach you that all composers have a favorite phrase or group of this kind which they use on all occasions, just as writers have a certain turn of phrase or painters a weakness to present some one feature always the same : for example, the clouds in Van de Velde's marine paintings.

The logical use of form in an artistic sense yields much power of construction, opposition, economy of thought, reminiscence and balance of parts. Every subject, then, must be rich in motive and capable of transformation and use in many settings as a whole. Next to his constructive power, and as the germ of it, Bach had a wonderful insight into the value of a theme. Everything he wrote proved that the theme could never be exhausted. The great power of his writing owes much to this one feature of keen discrimination in the construction of a subject. To-day you will find that there are more failures among students of composition, due to the one cause of no cultivation of judgment regarding the theme, than can be traced to aught else. No composition can have any value that is built on a meaningless subject. Given a theme pregnant with suggestive material, a composer has before him the most potent means of putting his thought in a lasting form. It is what we commonly call sticking to the subject that gives one's work a value. The theme that is full of suggestive material gives forth, when employed to best advantage, unity and economy of thought. It is precisely unity and economy of thought that stamps a work as coming from a well-trained mind, but to live, the work must unite besides these two features one other—a rich inspiration taken at its best.

Form always proclaims its own value and, on the contrary, no evidence of it is universally felt even though the want may not be explained by every one. It springs from nature, is found in nature's works, makes its way into every nook and corner of life and is the very body of art-work. How it is that music students can for years play the works of all great composers and never once chance to hear or to discover that music is given shape after laws governed by the same principles that build the cathedral, shape the richly wrought panel, shaft and capital, adorn the rood-screen and

fill the spandrel with magnificent figures in ornamentation, is, to say the least remarkable.　Not to
see Form in art is never to look upon the diamond
save in the rough.

"Once it was much to have found a practicable
way through the woods, but now every leaf on the
trees by the wayside must be counted; every stone
must be turned over to see if anything lies concealed beneath it." *

----

* Herman Grimm.

CHAPTER XVI.

SOME SPECIAL STUDIES IN MUSIC.

We don't work enough for the sake of learning, but too much for the sake of having it known that we work. The desire to excel is natural and commendable, but we must cut it down, and sacrifice ourselves in order to learn.

WILLIAM MORRIS HUNT.

Look well about you in the music world and you will discover that the majority of musicians are not educated, save in a very narrow sense, by the art work they carry on. As it is commonly studied music is not sufficient mental training. We make it appeal rather to undetermined sensations than to a well defined intellectual purpose. Thus you will discover that little good comes from music in the way of true education; which by the way is not mere knowledge-gathering. With a love for music that is decidedly an unknown quantity, too many of us are content to worship the speculative in the art of tone and never endeavor to find out positively what we are doing. There is in all art so much of reality, so much truth, beauty and wisdom for study and guidance, that I feel it to be well nigh a wrong to have to mention what is so true.

It is almost inconceivable that so many teachers

can be found in the arts whose conception of work is wrong throughout. Of its meaning and fitness in life they know nothing; they are either given to no thought at all or they are unsystematic in their thinking; they pay all heed to the gain and never think for a moment what art should do for them *as men and women;* which is the question that precedes all others. If one is earnest before them concerning these matters they smile good-naturedly or weariedly and wonder how you can moralize so; for their part, they go on their thoughtless way, leaving the door open every night, so that success may get in without trouble if it chances along before morning. They believe in balloons, because balloons go up. They do not think, however, that balloons go up only because they are light.

We are a nation of players and singers. Is that enough? "You would be astonished to hear how high I can sing!" says an enthusiastic one. "Oh, no I should not. How high you can sing simply excites my curiosity, and that is not the purpose of art. If you are to astound me at all it will be by the amount of soul you put in the range of voice which you have absolutely under control; if you cannot make me forget by your song that you are singing there yet remains something to be done." I present this picture to you only because I see how very prone art learners are to get effects by false means; by passing off bigness for greatness; and surface brilliancy for force and depth of meaning.

Here is one who laments that she does not succeed in teaching as she expected: with the most remarkable indulgence to herself she never thinks when she can avoid it, she counts on her fingers, teaches others exactly what she has been taught, avoids all endeavor in her lesson-giving, and yet puts great expectations in the least possible amount of activity; I tell her of her fault; she thinks she recognizes the wrong and promises to be more conscientious in the future; little suspecting that I recognize all her weakness in these few words. She does not know that the place for conscientiousness in doing the task lies years and years behind her. It should be the starting point; it always makes me sad to see any one heading towards it; I know there is something inherently wrong. Every good that has come to the world has been the result of earnestness in one form or another. There is no reason why, to the general fund of good, each one shall not add his part. What I am anxious to have you instill into others is this; it is a deep wrong to live and not contribute to the common welfare. Once get your students to understand this and art will be quite a different matter to them; they will turn attention to its earnestness, will begin to study its serious, lasting phases.   Once they begin this they are in a way to accomplish unknown good.   They will learn and honor the difference between a man of use and a public plaything.   They will not only make up their minds to do something but they will do it.

Now as to the Special Studies in Music, what are they?   I will give you some hints respecting them and let you do the work.   That is the best way for you.   When you have found something by your observation bring it to me and we will talk it over.   Most all people instinctively listen to music.   Why?   Music occupies a great place in the world; greater, perhaps, in the world of thought than in the world of pleasure.   Here then we have music fulfilling two functions, one high the other lower.   Consequently the nature of music must be very extensive; it evidently is necessary to both the serious and pleasurable phases of life, and whatever can appeal to the highest sense in life must be worth thinking about.   Be a thoughtful listener to music; study its effect upon yourself; if music is a language, as every one says, its messages should not forever be absolutely mist-hidden.   Think about this.

Sometimes the laymen want to know if there is money in music that so induced the master-composers to write their great works.   It is at all times amusing to watch the little mind fooling with a big topic; when little art makes big pretensions it is hard to keep the fool's cap out of sight. So you may ponder on this, though I hope there is no doubt in your minds concerning it : what makes low art? the low artist, the low clamoring public, or will art be expressed low as well as high? It is merely to decide whether good be purified evil or evil debased good.

Art has a tendency—very strong at times—where does it get it? Generations of learned people produce one writer. What has made art of to-day romantic? Why did it not forever stay as Bach left it? We are fond of comparing art to a mountain which we climb. It is not a good picture. Art is a river, flowing onward to eternity, and all we fail to know about it, is where and whither it may turn next. Whence it comes thither it returns.

Art is one voice for man. Man is a feeble voice of the nation in which he lives; the nation is but a flower of the time, and the time, however great it may be, is scarcely a moment in eternity. That reduces individual endeavor to its lowest terms, but it is a beginning in the chain of events, a link that must be; hence its value. Pin-holes in a sheet of paper give a child a fair idea of the stars; but one must, nevertheless, turn the telescope to the sky.

"Conscientiousness and justice," says the artist, William Hunt, "are stations which have been

reached and passed before any fine work appears."
Study in art those personalities that come before
you, study them carefully and you will group them
this way :—

Seventy-five per cent. work a little while on the
novelty of the task.

Twenty-four per cent., plus, are forever getting
ready to begin.

The rest are in earnest.

I have asked you to study the personality of the
artist *because that is the artist.* How he draws or
paints, sings or plays matters less; think of *him*
first, and afterwards of what he can do. Art
teaches the philosophy of life. Look among music
students of any station and you will be astonished
to discover the variations in the philosophy of life.
They have to educate the mind, the ear and the
hand. (I should have said soul, mind, ear and
hand.) How do they pay heed to these four demands ? This way—hand first, hand second, hand
third ; the rest fourth, and not too willingly. Some
discern the futility of that combination, and try
this—mind first, mind second, mind third, and the
remainder fourth ; but there are yet other combinations. [I want to say here, parenthetically,
that there is no sense so little cultivated by music
students in general as the sense of hearing. They
hear by sight, and so become musical deaf mutes.

There are very few *listeners* among the thousands of concert-attendants in the music centres; they drink in music because it is a form of intoxication for which they have contracted a weakness.]

It is surprising to know on how small a capital the business of life is carried by this little man and that. To be successful in warfare a nation must carry for arms not a long lance but a short sword. No one wants your long story full of promises, but a brief statement of substantial realities. That makes the best starting point for an investigation.

CHAPTER XVII.

THE SISTER ARTS.

The genial poet whose thought opens my talk with you only repeated what was expressed many years ago by Ludwig Holberg, the Norse Dramatist, and no one knows how many times by others: "A change of study is as grateful to the mind as a variety of grain is favorable to the fertility of the earth." Ruskin, too, expressed the necessity of this variety when he said to students of art: "Landscape can only be enjoyed by cultivated persons; and it is only by music, literature and painting that cultivation can be given." An American artist whose name is undoubtedly familiar to you has written: "People learn to love nature through pictures." I have repeated old truths to you so many times that if I keep on doing so you must forgive me in remembering that it is my intention to turn your thoughts into channels that will make you discover in music a beautiful reality, not an idealistic fancy.

Hence I have thought it worth while to talk in a general way of a few other beautiful realities to know which will make music truer, dearer and infinitely better in your sight.

"Art has grown through the centuries with the development of man's imaginative and artistic powers." Music is only one of the evidences of this result, and manifestly to become an artist one has need to inquire what may have been the scope and variety in the development of these powers; to know them in their fulness, makes stronger any special application of them that may be made, as it is by you, for example, in music. In Fine Art study of the most general nature you can gather so many hints of value in music that it is absolutely surprising that in music teaching there has not been outlined some work of good tendency for pupils to carry on in conjunction with their studies. It is true that in America comparatively little museum study of Fine Arts can be carried on except in a few large cities; and there, of course, the opportunities are far less than in European capitals. Yet there is so much to be done even here that one can gain an extensive general knowledge of many art subjects; thereby one of two gains results :—

(*a*) Either a better preparation is laid for a future European residence; or,

(*b*) If no European residence is possible one

has at least a general view of the art-field as it stretches about him. That very few students gain even what knowledge they might gather here is abundantly evident. Of the music students who go to our cities for study extending from one to three, four, or more years, very few take logical and studious advantage of putting into effect the very study they could be helped by to the most good. The fault is not wholly their own, and yet any inquiring mind, it seems, would find a way for solving little difficulties. There is to-day, and there will be for many years yet, much disregard paid by American students of music to the essential studies that must be pursued aside from music and yet hand and hand with it. Nevertheless the fact of their necessity is not the less true, and the truth of it is not in the least affected by any disregard that may be paid to it. Musical education is rushed; we fail to see that we do not reach the level of the mountain summit by climbing a tree at its foot; and yet we think the tree is very tall. I only wish that they who get to the top of it would tumble and be thrust along the way they should go. It is less surprising than curious to watch the antics of some students who leave home to study in an educational centre; they do not entertain the idea that hard work is a necessity; as a theoretic matter it serves as a

momentary impulse, but that is all. As for learning anything outside of music, that is a union of
parts in which they see no logic whatever. Any
attempt to bring it well before them as a necessity
produces the same effect as to touch an open
bivalve; the shell closes like a vise. But hundreds
of students are willing and anxious to work at all
one may find good for them, and it is for the sake
of them that the instructor should assign from time
to time some lessons in the study of paintings,
statues, prints, pottery, glass, coins, designs, and
the like, provided he can do so to the student's
advantage as an artist in music. The special work
every student does will readily suggest what
practical side-study of art may be carried on.
What is the gain? Why the possible gain is so
great that I cannot begin to tell you what it is.
Chief of all, you will *conceive* better the general
lesson of art and feel more forcibly its eternal
truth. Truth and beauty in art are more keenly
felt, more fully comprehended as absolute qualities
when one learns to trace their application in many
forms of art. The various applications one meets
with are more likely to provide the suggestiveness
of art than a single topic alone. For you must not
lose it to sight that you are or ought to be not
merely musicians but artists; instructors not of
music alone but of art, and any of you who are

hoping to fulfill the pedagogical needs of to-morrow must keep the matter constantly in mind.

I know very well that this study requires time, not only for the actual doing of it but for the consideration of how to do it and how to apply it; but it is time you can and must afford to take. Do you remember what Mendelssohn said: " I thus saw the truth confirmed, that perfection, even in a sphere the most foreign to us, leaves its own stamp on the mind." This stamp or impression is all the more forcibly made when it is gathered in as a power from the many streams which are the tributaries of the river of art. I have said that by this logical nomadism you will conceive music better, and the reason is this,—you will find that the special principles underlying music are not arbitrary demands of pedantry but special application of broad laws that make the substructure of all art. The better one conceives these laws in their broadest sense the better he will apply them in a special way. To effect this you are not to understand that I think it necessary for the young musician to strive to become landscape painter, poet, sculptor or builder, but I do mean that all these lines of thought touch his and have something in common with the music he tries to interpret. What he is to find out is how much knowledge of these things he needs and how to get it; then, further, he must get it and give it application. In this sense I should like to see you become students of these subjects, have your hour or two now and then in the museums, study fine buildings, and do not forget nature. There are many instructive books on this general study that it would certainly be of worth for you to look through and to study if you can find the time. At the end of this talk I shall name some which you may see and judge for yourself.

Do not think as you read this that you are to set about doing it all at once. Had you given it heed daily—or even less frequently—for four or five years past you would know much about the topic to-day. What you may have done you may yet do. My only wish is that you incorporate this line of thought and of inquiry into your work. In thus multiplying the objective points for your lines of inquiry in art you are not digressing, you are simply putting more facets to the gem. I do not believe in mixing studies, for, as Roger Ascham says: "If you put malveseye and sack, redde wyne and white, ale and beere, and all in one pot, you shall make a drinke not easye to be known nor yet holesome for the bodye." All the study you can do, however, to the broadening of the one theme which you have made your own must be decidedly "holesome for the bodye," and I would not see you afraid to undertake it. Get close to music and to art in general, yet do not fail to acquire the power of throwing your work off into the distance where you can see it better. You know how the artists look at a picture by making a little frame of the hand; everything "stands out" better then. I like to indulge in mental perspective; one sees so much that way. This thought has been well expressed by a writer in a paper on Jean François Millet, the French peasant painter; speaking of how one should look at certain pictures, Millet " insisted that the pictures should be seen at a considerable distance, say at four or five times their greatest width or height, but (and this is a suggestive act) called me near sometimes that I might see the simplicity of execution or the few touches it required in producing multiplicity and infinity in effect." *

A little nomadism in art is apt to impress it upon you that the wisest plan is to build slowly. If by adding a little wheel now and then to the mechanism of the educational machine you thereby increase the motive power, by all means add it. Many side-studies in art may not, directly in themselves, be of interest and value to you, but there are many that strike a wonderfully suggestive parallel with

---

* Wyatt Eaton.

music study, which makes you think that the kin-
ship of the fine art family is very close.   Art being
the most beautiful representation of the truth, it
follows that one sees in music and pictures, poetry
and statues only different idioms of expression.
We have here not four arts, but four outlets for art
thought.   All expression of thought by art-means
is not an endeavor to make something beautiful to
the eye, but it is such an embodiment of something
truthful and beautiful within, as will raise in others
the emotions of the one who so expresses himself.
" It is not the eye that sees the beauties of heaven,
nor the ear that hears the sweetness of music, or
the glad tidings of a prosperous accident; but the
soul that perceives all the relishes of sensual and
intellectual perceptions: and the more noble and
excellent the soul is, the greater and more savory
are its perceptions." *   When the art work comes
from one who has little within, the work possesses
little in itself and appeals to equally as little in
others.   One cannot bring forth what the character
does not inspire, and it may further be said that
expression is seldom if ever equal to the conception that prompts it.   Why the great army of
painters, composers and writers are doomed to

---

* Jeremy Taylor.

failure is either because their work is imitative and has value only as a copy more or less faithful, or it is hoped for it that it will appeal to more in others than there is in the soul of him who executed it.*

---

* The works referred to in this chapter are added at the end of this volume.

CHAPTER XVIII.

TASTE AND TOLERANCE.

If there is one characteristic which marks taste and refinement in a nation, it is a love for nature and the beauties which adorn it.—MARCUS B. HUISH, LL.B.

How many of you have thought that the history of art in a nation is paralleled time and time again by the history of the growth and love of art in the individual?   This is true; a representative man is the key to his time; all its phases and changes are found in him; his development gives one the clew to the advancement of the time; all that pertains to the people is found in him, but more rapidly consummated, more deeply felt, more plainly to be traced. As truly as it was written that many centuries of salon life and brilliant conversation were required to make possible a Madame de Staël, so with equal truth it is to be said that to produce an artistic people, decades of writers, painters, builders, composers, men of all forms of intellectual training, must pour forth their life and work to be as everlasting lesson-themes to any willing learner who may come to the altar where they have worshipped. The art of Europe to-day is simply the story of its artists.

To become artistic the thought must go out to the beautiful, question it, learn it and interpret it. After the day of Use comes the day of Use combined with Beauty; later on Beauty is accepted for itself alone; then it is questioned, systematized, and from it is evolved the science of its nature. Education in art makes few of us keen observers; we become either the pedant or the hypocrite. By this I mean that besides the artist who is thoroughly equipped by nature and training for filling the art-place he occupies to great advantage, there are two other classes; one, that makes art a school-room, and the other that apes the wisdom and devotion of some one ahead whom he has secretly selected to himself as a leader. Without discussing the respective merits of these three classes, it may be said of them that each seems to get what the others do not. One creates in art, the second is scholastic about it, the third chases it in every direction, either because he likes the sport or ultimately hopes to catch something. If it were possible, I would like to know how many of three thousand listeners of a series of Symphony Concerts receive :—

(*a*) Any actual instruction from what they hear, or

(*b*) Any definite idea of what pure instrumental music means, or

(*c*) A just estimate of the labor reaching from the present to the far past, that gives them the enjoyment they are tolerant enough to take provided a comfortable seat and similar accessories are not wanting.

Further I should like to weigh the intelligence of each of them from year to year, compliment some of them on their gain and try to force a confession from the others. We would first have to understand each other then we could enjoy the result.

Tell me, is it Taste or Tolerance that makes this young woman an art-amateur? She needs to do nothing, because it happens to be her misfortune to be wealthy. To pass the time she is required to study two languages, devote a morning every week to painting, and two hours a week to instruction in music, besides following other employments that, in her life, fill rather the niche of fashion than of use. She does nothing well in any of these subjects; speaks with a slur about the noblest music that can be put before her if her technic happens to fall short of performing it, which it invariably does. Any of the five or more lessons she receives are put off when, and as frequently as may be desirable if a trifling event requires it; she is infinitely above anything that may be taught her, and regards the whole circle of her enforced activity either as a bore or with the complacency of the king who notices that the fool is present.

Nothing can reach the real personality in her, hence she always remains neutral or worse. She expects no influence to be exerted beyond that of making matters as comfortable as can be for her. She buys that consideration and naturally expects to get it. This is drawn from life, and it is not her fault altogether that she is what she is.

While ignorant defiance of the truth of art is not synonymous with toleration it may come very near to being so. It must be evident to all that art is extensively tolerated because the dictates of fashion make it proper. The most stupid and amusing conversation to be heard anywhere is to be heard in galleries and concert halls. It is not taste that drives the public in the presence of art so much as it is the desire to follow the leadership of some one who knows how valuable such things are—and thus seem to have individual liking for them. An extremely interesting writer on Natural History, Mr. J. G. Wood, has been honest enough to say something about the dulness of museums. When we are perfectly honest with each other concerning this matter of art may not some of the laymen write interestingly concerning the dulness of pictures and symphonies?

Not long since I made an inquiry, experimentally —of three attendants at the same Symphony

Concert—" How was you impressed by this particular concert ?"   The first person replied :—

—" The Overture was played magnificently; I do not recall a better performance; indeed it was so good that I went out immediately after this number (the first) for fear another would spoil the impression !"

The second :—

—" Infernally bored but stuck it out.   Glad there's only a few more in this series ! "

The third :—

—" Oh it was so charming, you know.   How life-like it is in the—well I've forgotten the number, where the thunder comes in."

[Did Beethoven try to make the thunder *life-like ?*]

Taste gave me the first answer and two forms of Tolerance gave me the others; the second was stupid tolerance and the third was indifferent tolerance. Just how far it may be fair to criticise Toleration in educational matters we will not discuss, but it is very true that much of the attention bestowed is not from appreciation but from a spirit of patronage. Sometimes the character is mistaken, just as we fail to recognize our friends at a masquerade, but the mask is soon dropped and we all laugh over the mistakes. We admit our children to education of various kinds with the vague idea that it will benefit them—how we do not know. Too much art is studied this way. It is somewhat to be regretted because such learners do not in some cases have any impulse to seek anything in the matter; they remain passive because that is the easiest way to make the obligation light. Nothing is of so little satisfaction to any instructor as to teach art as an educational ornament. They have to be pleased rather than taught; a very little gilding must be spread over a base metal and polished as if it were rich to the core. Such art-counterfeiting should be punished or prohibited. But I say nothing of the amateur in this connection save that he must have the same talent and as strong application as his professional brother. They differ only in the *use* to which they put their learning not in the manner of getting it: which must be the same for all—so much work and so much gain according to the strength of the worker. But so curious has the use of these terms become that "amateur" is frequently applied to any one who knows a little regarding a special topic toward which he may have some pretensions. Stated broadly, any one who makes money from art, letters, or science is a "professor."

I have, a moment ago, spoken to you of an experimental inquiry—here is another. I ask an intellectual man who is a natural lover of the beautiful why low attempts in art become popular?

—" Because there is little or no thought in them."

I ask some one else the same question in a different form :—

"Why is it that the finest of art does not become popular?"

—" O, it comes too high, people can't stand the expense."

CHAPTER XIX.

MORE ABOUT BOOKS AND READING.

Je prends Condillac. Sais-tu ce que j'en ai lu en cinq heures? Vingt pages.
—*Poinsot à Michlet.*

I find it is a great deal to begin with if a book so far attracts us that we resolve, without urging, to look it through; since, as a measure of self-preservation, it is necessary to stand on the defensive now-a-days against books and people, if we would reserve time and inclination for our own thoughts.
—HERMAN GRIMM.

The book of to-day, in fine binding, with letters and designs in black and gold, of finest paper and faultless impression of type and illustration, is a marvel of luxury beside that which the Saxons named a *bôc*. Do you know what it means, this word *book* of ours? On the Teutonic side of our speech we find, in at least half-a-dozen languages, that the form changes very little. Look at the forms *bôc*, *bôk*, *bok*, *bog*, *boek*, *buch*; each means a *book*, and our own word is similar to them all. The Anglo-Saxon parent of our word-form is the first quoted above, *bôc*, a derivative from

201

the noun *bôce*, meaning a beech-tree. It was on beechen boards that our Teutonic ancestors committed their writing. Knowing this, one is pleased at the contrast between the magnificent volumes of a modern library and the beechen chronicle of our northern forefathers.   I have just used another word to which I will ask you to give attention before we enter into this talk; it is *library*. This is the book-word of the Southern nations, and runs through many of them, as you will see in the forms I quote: *liber, librarius, librari, libraire, librero, librarium, librajo.*

In our own tongue we see how the word-form of the north has come down and that of the south come up to us; and we have the word color of two climes in our language. So when we say *book*, the Saxon beech-tree comes to mind; and when, to convey the idea of many books collected in one place, we say *library*, the Latin form comes to us. But I love the Saxon form the more; it is so typical of the race; it is a word from the lips of nature, just as our Gothic Cathedral is a picture in stone of the forest. "The Gothic church plainly originated in a rude adaptation of the forest trees with all their boughs to a festal or solemn arcade, as the bands about the cleft pillars still indicate the green withes that tied them. No one can walk in a road cut through pine woods, without being struck with the architectural appearance of the grove, especially in winter, when the bareness of all other trees shows the low arch of the Saxons. In the woods in a winter afternoon one will see as readily the origin of the stained glass window with which the Gothic cathedrals are adorned, in the colors of the western sky seen through the bare and crossing branches of the forest." *   Everywhere we find nature giving hints to man. He wanders through the forest and she turns his thoughts to church-building, so he becomes an adept in the arts of design, of proportion, of ornament, and of construction. She sets him scribbling his thoughts on beechen boards; the beechen boards must be kept together, and for centuries he goes on learning his lesson better and better, calling in as he can other arts, sciences, and manufactures to help him. In time he has formulated a certain amount of knowledge concerning this work, the fruit of his observation, and this knowledge is the art of book-making. Its evolution is worth tracing, and if you trace it only in the faintest lines let me ask you some time to be so curious as to know something of the wonderful biography of books. It will be to you an interesting tale, and you will love all the more these dear

----

* " Essay on History," R. W. Emerson.

friends of our solitude that light up life and all
the world with their cheer and wisdom.

In the first talks we had together I spoke to you
of books in the home. I hope there is not one of
you who has not in the house a few volumes that
are in every sense your property, bought with
money you have earned, read and learned in hours
you have found for them aside from your employment. I care not how few or many are your books
if only you know them by your own exertion.
You are busy musicians, therefore I know you to
have but limited opportunity for dwelling in a
library, but I expect to find you owners of small
but very wisely chosen book collections. That is
the ideal of book ownership; every member of the
collection should be as wisely chosen as a friend.
You will make, too, acquaintances in your reading
days—but own the friends, and let these others
prove themselves before they are admitted as one
of you. The best libraries of the future will be
those small collections of books, gathered with extreme care by the specialist and constantly tested;
in which there is found not a single volume that is
not of intrinsic worth in every word, and which
may be quite as inexhaustible as a store of wisdom
at the end of half a century's continued friendship
as in the first days. Think for a moment what an
inexhaustible mine of good thought may be put

into any fireside bookcase of smallest dimensions. On the bottom shelf there should be found :—

1. The Bible.
2. Shakespeare.
3. Dante.
4. Bunyan.
5. Milton.
6. Goethe.

On the next above :—

7. Plutarch.
8. Emerson.
9. Locke.
10. Descartes.
11. Plato.
12. Spenser.

On the next there would be these writers of history and romance :—

13. George Eliot.
14. Sir Walter Scott.
15. Björnstjerne Björnson.
16. Victor Hugo.
17. George Ebers.
18. George MacDonald.

Of companionable, chatty writers :—

19. Hugh Miller.
20. Samuel Smiles.
21. Dr. Holmes.
22. John Lubbock.

And for the top :—

23. Hans Christian Andersen.
24. Longfellow.
25. Martin Luther's Table-talk.

Here is a library of only twenty-five authors; it offers something to every taste. Every author is deservedly famed, and while, taken as a whole, they may offer no consistent worth to any reader, it is not difficult to select from them many a single work that would make one a most formidable " man of one book." I would like to see in every home, not this library, for I do not flatter myself that it is a collection that any one would find correctly formed, but one made on similar lines, and I feel free to say that none of you will see your own or any other home library wisely formed *that does not contain some of them.* This shows that as in every age some men and women rise like mountain peaks above the rest, so above all the books to which we have access some are seen afar off, looming above their fellows, some are mere undulations, others are swamp and morass. It is the mountain peak you must aim for, traveling on the way over the undulating plain, but not forever dwelling there.

In the two talks that follow we are to speak of books in special connection with our work as musicians; here we have to do with what is the property of the world at large. True books are the songs of the human soul, and as such they belong to all men alike; therefore the inheritance that is yours is certainly worth looking after, and, having once established your claim, you should certainly get all that belongs to your strength. The exclusiveness of the music-life is sufficient for you; I only hope sincerely that it is not too much so for your best interest. By no means do I hint that music is a world too small for you; what I mean is this: if you do not, now and then, pitch your tent outside its domains I fear you will mistake its great world for a workshop, wherein you should labor all day for an all-day pay and then go home out of it.   That you are not dwellers in such restricted quarters I would have you believe on my assurance, if that were enough; but by all means it is not.   You can only learn by learning.   Precisely why I would have you read and write as much as I have recommended is because I know you will, thereby, learn the sooner to quit your dreaming.   Until then you do not know the market-value of reality.   To-day's army of art-instructors is a unique feature of the history of these times.   Never before has the close-knitting of the world of art and the world outside of art been so clearly displayed.   It has never before been so commonly known how much close relationship the artist and his outer world must have for their mutual benefit.   And now I may say, in self-explanation, the reason I have put before you in both series of these talks, so very much to do lying not in music but upon its confines, is because I am absolutely certain that it will quicken the art-sense within you or prove to you that you have almost none.   In the one instance it would materially help you onward; in the other, it would teach you the wisdom of earning bread out of art, and of spending your spare minutes in its service if you cannot keep away from it. The sooner you learn the difference between a talent for art and what may be a passing fancy for it, the better for you, as a useful man or woman. It is an unpleasant statement for me to make to you, but it is certainly true, that there are too many misfits in art who are wasting their time and, by their misplaced activity, setting art in a false light. So you see how true it is that much of the strength of the true artist is lost in combating the evil of his neighbor. Why I would have you all become as early as possible students of other matters than art is now clearly defined; if you are an artist it will make you a better one; if you are not it will soon tell you so. It is in nature and in literature that you can best wander to the end that you may measure your own strength; in nature, because that is a most inexhaustible world of forms and of divine laws; in literature, because that is the best record of man's thought for ages past.

Whatever be your station in art-work you may be assured that to whatever height you go in your labor you will crave to mount as high in other worlds. If you have a well-schooled intelligence for the classical in one art you will be led to the same in all others, and to the same in the world of letters. The reason thereof is plain enough; the mind recognizing and craving a high ideal in one form of beauty most naturally seeks to recognize the same in another form to which it may turn. Knowing two languages equally well, a man does not read high thoughts in one and low thoughts in the other. Thus I feel that in wandering in the wonder-world of nature and in the wonder-world of literature you will very soon strike your art-level. Having done that you have both oriented and measured yourself as well to others as to yourself.

It is now plain that when I demand seriousness in your reading it is only because I would have you know from the beginning that you must be everywhere and at all times up to your level as an artist; if this is not so, you are not the artist you think yourself. Thus literature, nature, and science are to you simply other dialects of the art language which is your mother tongue, and, as I have said before, I cannot imagine you to read high thought in the one and low thought in another. There is a certain candor of mind, a gravity in dealing with trifles, that always defines the man. He cannot be all truth here and part truth there; he must be all truth or untruth everywhere.

I would, then, have you go to your books with earnestness because you must be earnest in art to become artists—or rather let me explain and say that one cannot become an artist, for the artist is always there, he simply develops. You will read your volumes as you read the phases of your daily art-work, deeply. You will recognize those to be well-read who have read well. Some one very pertinently said: " It is one thing to read a book because we want to get through it, and another thing to be through with it because we want to read it. A well-reading man thinks less of getting through a book than of getting a book through him. It is better wholly to read half a good book than to half read a whole one." It is everywhere that old, well-worn, homely truth which you will weary of before you comprehend—it is the earnestness of the man that tells.

A gallery of portraits of readers would be amusing instruction. Here is one who reads everything; like a bottle, his mind will hold anything one may turn into it, but it never becomes a better bottle. Here is another so painfully exact that he stays too close to his subject to understand its unity. Like the ant that climbs the cherry tree, it cannot see the cherry tree because it climbs it. This one does not know that to recognize the beauty of a flower you must get close to it; but to conceive the grandeur of a mountain chain you must wander until it is far behind. A third reads nothing in the whole because he is constantly finding another book better than the one he has, and so he nibbles first at this, then at that, all the while smiling with toleration at the enthusiast of one book or of one author. And so on through the whole gallery; I need not describe them further; keep your observation keen and you will find the others for yourselves.

There are all characteristics in books, because these characteristics are in men who write. So we class them as excitant and soporific, irritant and sedative, according as they work upon us, or rather according as they convey those states of being from the writer to the reader. " There is no calamity in this world," says Ludwig Holberg, " which literature cannot in some measure contribute to alleviate." It is to win from books this influence, that we approach them. The power of a book is its magnetism, a subtle cause of action that is plain enough but which cannot be explained. I would recommend that you become close students of the parentage of books; therein is the secret of their coloring matter. You will see how very few of them are really the offspring of good intention. The best are endlessly repeated or assailed or imitated, and in time one finds that the best reading, when reduced to its lowest terms, is not a very great quantity. More than you can know may be ranged along the walls of your music-room, though

it be a small one.   Thus the utility of a great library
to a schooled reader is parallel with the utility of
the reference-book to the student, to be used when
needed.   The library should supply a reader's wants
but not create them.   When you begin to wonder
what you should read next, read nothing ; in the
meantime observe and think ; you will be all the
brighter for the abstinence.

Every new book—new to you—which is added
to the library of your intelligence is another carat
to its worth.   It is nothing more, but that is a great
deal.

CHAPTER XX.

A LIBRARY—HOW TO MANAGE IT.

There are no scales in which to weigh culture.
The great books of the world, like the stars, shine only here and there, but the zenith has them as well as the nadir.—Dr. Geikie.

It is one thing to have a library; another to know how best to use it. To the experience necessary to enable one to use a small library well one must add that which is necessary to deal with large collections. Book using is now an art, for books are tools, and tools to be used efficiently must be used with skill. The multiplication of books is one of the many results that have followed in the wake of the printer's and book-maker's art. The publishers and the writers would give us no respite but constantly thrust upon us not only a great number but a great variety of works,—so it has become an art to choose from all they put before us a little of the best and let the rest pass on, to choose a little and, having a need for it, make the most of it. As from among all the people that surround us we must gather first acquaintances then friends, so we must select here a book to know passingly, there another to cherish as a life-long friend and be content to let the rest go by or maybe learn of them by observation or by chance.

There are very few educated people who do not find rest, help, and deep inspiration in some one volume. In the history of every reader there should be famed volumes, famed to him who reads them. They are history makers. "Some books are edifices to stand as they are built; some are hewn stones ready to form a part of future edifices; some are quarries from which stones are to be split for shaping and after use." The great books are those that should sink deepest into our lives; the edifice-building books, those that "do preserve, as in a phial, the purest efficacy and extraction of that living intellect that bred them." *

The value of a library is not its size but its depth. It can show only what we are or what we have been. Very often when reviewing our book possessions we find volumes that we have outrun; their worth is as nothing to us because somewhere or in something else we have found more than they are. Hence one comes to believe in library-weeding; in putting aside, though it may not be out of possession, the books of yesterdays. "The libraries of young men are largely filled with books which they will be ashamed of after a few years."? †

---

* Milton.   † Dr. Geikie.

Books in a library are like ore in the mine—raw material, the raw material of thought,—to gain any good from it, one must work it patiently. But there is a difference—the ore of metal is not increased, however carefully it is worked, but the more one dwells with thought the more it goes on multiplying in power and extent; and increasing, too, in the sterling value of its worth. [You must not charge me with a lack of definiteness for not having said that this thought of which we are speaking should be " good" thought. I do not see why we should qualify our speech by adjectives that show we mean well. If, when one says " thought" you give as much heed to the possible evil as the good thereof, the misfortune is yours.] Do not be for-ever reading. Be frequently bookless, sit and think ; not a guess, now and then, but true meditation, makes the man. Wisdom is not the bright saying you chance upon but the truth you have discovered by delving in your own thoughts. Books never supply thought · they move it. They are thought incentives ; not its substitutes. The power of a printed word is unlimited ; that is why one should display the greatest wisdom in the selection of his books. " We need to be as careful of our printed as of our living companions." It is the friendship, the companionability of books that makes it worth our while to own them. Whoever has in his home a book of truth, of value and of deep worth, entertains a right royal guest; can he think too highly of it? honor it too much? This deep and true friendship for literature cannot then be centered upon very many objective points. Leaving out of our consideration books that are merely pleasure giving, the number of useful volumes we can collect and know thoroughly is very small. I think, in consequence, that this statement is true: the more education spreads the smaller private libraries will become. The wisest recommendation, then, would seem to be, prefer to have small, wisely chosen libraries for your special work. As you gather your books with care, watch them, also, in like manner. A book that is capable of teaching you for many years, that continues to prove your friend and counsellor, is surely worth a little attention.

I will not give any special hints concerning shelf arrangement, because wall space, size of room, and a number of other considerations tend to make this a question each must solve independently. But there is this much to be said: If books form any important part of your working tools they should be just as easily reached as possible. Hence, in providing a place for them, let it be the most convenient you can command. When you have determined where your book-shelves shall be, consider this very simple point—in all collections of books some are most frequently used, used continually; these should be placed in the most convenient part of your book-cases.   Even in so simple a matter as this if one avails of all advantageous points he will find that they contribute a great deal in their totality toward simplifying his means of action; and whatever does that saves time, and whatever saves time lengthens life.

Private libraries for practical working purposes should be small, but this does not mean you should debar yourself from the ownership of volumes that find a purpose apart from enlightening you in your own work.   Let me give it to you as a hint, that you can do a grain of good here and there by placing, judiciously, good books in the hands of students who have not yet learned to read to a purpose.   Let it be a part of your education to keep well-informed concerning books that have value as *first reading*, books chiefly inspirational. They are mind openers, and you will find that they are not merely a help to him who reads them but to you, for they will have made for you a better student.   To practical teachers this knowledge of readable books for all classes of art-students is indispensable.   If you own these volumes you can readily place them in the proper hands; it will be much better than merely to recommend them, because the volume advised is not always looked up even after all you may have said in favor of it. You will find a great difference in students, both as to their inclination for reading and the benefit they gather from it; any book, however, that inspires a mind must have its good influence, and of such volumes you should certainly have knowledge. I may say, too, that you will find it to require no little knowledge of human nature on the one hand and of literature on the other before you can put the right book in the right hands.

If your students are not accustomed to books make them so as soon as possible. It is not simply curious, but remarkable, how many art-students there are who know nothing whatever about manipulating books. There is not one of them in a score or more who can get anything out of a great library if you should turn him loose in it. Another phase of the students' book-life, which all you instructors must have noticed, is this—students will spend two years, more or less, in study away from home, in the art centre they think best for them; they have an indistinct impression that a great library might be of service; they find there is one which they may use; they know, too, that the books they should read from this library are those specially helpful to them in their work, books that, from their special nature, are not found everywhere;

and what happens ?   They make a feeble attempt at finding what they want, lose interest because it costs a little trouble and promises to be hard reading, and capitulate with themselves so far as to read nothing but books of the lightest character which they might find in the library of any village that boasts a hundred or two volumes.   Yet many of these people can be turned into good readers by one who will take the trouble to force them gently into the proper way.   Now and then, however, there wanders into the teacher's experience an obdurate case; you lead him to the library, find him a place in good light and air, open the proper volume at the proper place, put your finger on the word at which he is to begin, turn to him and say all is ready, and—he has fallen asleep.   Such cases may be rare; when you chance upon one do your best upon it until you find that it must be dismissed with the same ceremony and reward as were be-stowed upon Gil Blas when, as a youth, he set out for Salamanque to buy wisdom with foolishness.

"There are no scales in which to weigh culture," therefore be slow to judge the reading of another who knows fewer books than you.   His library may have less in it than you find in your own but he may know deeply what he has.   The one valued part in reading is the thought that accompanies and pursues it.   Not pleasure alone must be the reader's object.   A library of books that are pleasing to the imagination but do not teach are simply the toys of an adult child—his box of mental playthings.   There are readers or book-gorgers who take in immense quantities of this and that, which is their intoxication.   As the drinker must have his liquor so they must have their cheap romance, to thrill, if it can, the brain that grows more stupid from day to day.   There is a leading thought, which is honesty to the self, that must be kept constantly in sight by the book-reader and by the book-buyer.   Do not admit to your library what you would not give to another in whom you have interest, as a true and helpful volume.

A little money goes a long way, in these days, in the purchase of books.   For the reader and teacher who makes books helpful, who finds them a necessity, volumes well-bound, well-printed from clear and good-sized type and convenient in form are the best.   Volumes that you can take to the fireside are the most companionable.   It is a safe rule to observe regarding book-purchase to avoid the cheapest and the very best, for these reasons : when a publisher sets out to make a book in a very cheap style he does it at the loss of its essentials; when he makes it a very expensive volume it is in the multiplication and over-elaboration of its unessentials.   On the one hand you do not wish to sacrifice to cheapness, usefulness in a volume, and on the other there is little use in paying over-much for very expensive bindings. It is too frequently true that the fine art of the book-binder makes more appeal than that which he richly attires.

Buy few, if any, books experimentally; first know something of them, then you may be sure if they are of any value to you or not. Provide yourself with some means for cataloguing your library, including reference to valuable articles in magazines. The objective point is to have the cream of all your reading always at command. It does not serve you to any purpose to read and forget; when you have read something of value you should never lose sight of it. A catalogue-reference in your library is good training in itself, it will teach you to give every book and magazine a place; there is no more useless possession than an orderless library.

In buying books be guided by common sense and your honest needs, not by the capriciousness of fancy; in caring for them look to convenience; in reading them look for all there is in them *and more too*.

When you enter a fine library you are in the throne-room of the earth's true kings. They will take up their abode in your dwelling; not only this but they are willing to serve you; so be worthy of their service. Do not forget that a library reflects the mind that makes it. One of the most genial characters in English fiction said a very true word for books in this wise: "I showed her that books were sweet, unreproaching companions to the miserable, and that if they could not bring us to enjoy life, they would at least teach us to endure it." *

---

* Goldsmith ("Vicar of Wakefield").

CHAPTER XXI.

IN AND OUT OF BOOKS.

No book is worth anything, which is not worth much; nor is it serviceable until it has been read, and re-read, and loved, and loved again, and marked, so that you can refer to the passages you want in it, as a soldier can seize the weapon he needs in an armory, or a housewife bring the spice she needs from her store. Bread of flour is good; but there is bread, sweet as honey, if we would eat it, in a good book; and the family must be poor indeed which cannot once in a while, for such multipliable barley-loaves, pay their baker's bill.— JOHN RUSKIN.

A man with ideas of value which you do not find in books is always an agreeable companion. He must not have run after his originality; it must be a part of him—or better still, it must be the essence of the man. No one can read the journals of Henry Thoreau without being impressed at every entry that Thoreau was greater than any book he could possibly write. It is curious that so many of us pay willing court to opinions in books that would never win our heed out of them. Whoever tries to think well should entertain his thought, for it is a noble guest. Is it not better first to have solved in your own mind what you read in books? I have said many warm words to you about books, and at my best I cannot tell you how much I cherish them for the joy and good and wisdom they contain; so what I have to say in this talk you must not interpret as against aught I have said in their praise; I must repeat that I could not praise them highly enough. But there is one thing else to which I want you to give at least an equal value with that which you set on reading: and that is observation ripened by thought.

In the first series of these talks I advised you to have side-studies; hobbies, if you will. I hope they have been of double advantage to you, namely, subjects aside from the art work you are engaged in, that will give you rest from the vocation and an opportunity to sharpen other faculties than those you employ in music. A healthful state of such activity is needful, or we would all lapse into that state of passive receptivity which you can find abundantly about you. In these days of thousands of books and millions of periodical publications we are unfortunate in the very possession of so much. Once we pay too much attention to it; once we lean too trustingly upon it, we have sacrificed the self and acknowledged a proxy. That is speedy death to the most gifted intelligence. Fortunately there is no branch of the study you must do as artists that does not admit of investigation, that is not a field, rich in what it offers to you as an observer.   In science accurate training of the powers of observation is so essential that no book knowledge is sufficient.   Consequently, scientific men attain an accuracy of thought and of the process of investigation that is remarkable.   This accuracy of thought becomes habitual to them, and they apply it everywhere.   Agassiz was one of the keenest observers; he recognized the value of his power to its fullest extent, and sought at once to make students aware of it.   It was better, in his opinion, to let " the pupil find in his daily walks the illustration and repeated evidence of what he has heard in the school-room."   Book and nature, but not book alone, is the principle.   When one studies nature, nature is the best book of illustration one can have; all others are commentary that are to be used only for what they are proved to be worth by the greater book and for nothing more.

It is worthy of notice that every scientist who has left us any evidences of his methods of work illustrates the one lesson I wish you to take—observation.   They did more with their eyes as they looked and pryed into the ways of nature, than by scanning scores of authors.   Miller, the Cromatry geologist, I have previously mentioned to you; readers of the charming autobiography of Arminius Vambéry, know how much he had to trust his

15

eyes and memory, because note-taking was almost impossible. "I seem to be one sent into the world to see and observe. . . . . In short, the joy of my heart is to study men, their manners and their ways." * There is nothing so valuable as information at first hand. You cannot get too much of it. The reason why scientific men are as a class accurate observers is, because science does not tolerate book-knowledge alone. A scientific man regards knowledge in a book as gathered fruit. He sets about finding out who picked it—when, where and how. After he is satisfied on these points he partakes of it, if it is necessary. Scientific knowledge of many kinds, that is recorded in books, has frequently but a short life, because of the discovery of new truths, the teachings of more complete generalizations and the adding of facts to facts which frequently alter the nature of previously formed conclusions. This never-ending activity that is required of the scientist, makes him a more skilled man to-morrow than he is to-day. He trusts his book for its relative value, knowing that a year hence, perhaps, it will be valueless to him. Recently the University of Edinburgh revised its scientific library. Sir James Simpson was asked what books on his specialty should be retained:

---

* Burns (Correspondence of).

"Take out every text-book that is more than ten years old, and put it down in the cellar," he said.*

I may be wrong in what I am about to say, but I have often thought that artists looked down on the exactness of science, regarded it as unworthy of notice, because of its lack of the poetic element, while art is to them the heaven of beauty. And it has likewise always occurred to me that the sooner artists recover from this feverish misconception and learn the truth of the matter, the better artists they will become. We can only pity in charity of feeling him who has found out that what he does is in all consideration the greatest of all things. Science and art of no kind can reach that place. It is a matter of wonder that so few of us discover how admirably adaptable in art are scientific teachings and methods. Greater, not lesser, art comes from the union. There is little fear for the genius; he is generally of clear thought. The little men suffer most from elevation. Dwelling in a tiny world they breathe quickly and attenuate the atmosphere. Breathing the air that surrounds them breeds the misconception which marks them for life. It is the loud and continued talk of these little folks which gives that awkward twist and turn to art by which many are led to misjudge its value, its place and its power.

---

* Prof. Drummond ("The Greatest Thing in the World ").

Everywhere in art you should keep your eyes open. Gather fruits of observation and group them. Isolated facts have little value. It is the grouping of them and deducing a law therefrom that gives them worth. Scientific investigation of certain phases of music has done very little yet; you need not have taught music long to discover this. In the matter of Musical Form, for example, I feel safe in saying that a keen, active mind given to accurate investigation and, further, having the faculty of generalizing and grouping what it learns, can gather more knowledge of the subject in a few years of active work, than is contained in all the literature we have of this topic And there are many other such themes for investigation.

Beautiful as art is in its every detail it is only valuable when thought of utmost accuracy underlies it. Dreaming produces nothing but dreamers. I would not have you so visionary that you can pin yourself to nothing. You must have faith in what you do, but not less faith in the health of yourself. When art produces it is in a healthful way. The parasites in art keep on soaring until they get dizzy; they rave over their journey and hold all mud-stained travellers in contempt. They are always dissatisfied, despite their equanimity. They smile at the world, to be sure, but better still the world laughs outright at them and is pleased to get along without their presence. "Art teaches you the philosophy of life, and if you can't learn it from art, you can't learn it at all ".* Art is a wonderfully great world. I only fear as I talk to you that I may not succeed in impressing you with this thought. It is not enough that you regard quietly what other men have done—*you must be doing*. Look at the world you live in and try to see in it what no one else has seen. Quietly to sit by and drink in for pleasure the thoughts of other men is merely a form of intoxication of which you should be ashamed to be found guilty. Every one of you with a mind, healthy thought, two eyes and the faculty for using them, can labor in the workshop of the world so well that what you have seen and heard and learned could not be found in volumes. This is the kind of men and women that is needed in art,—active, vigorous thinkers, careful of what they say but not afraid to speak when they know they are right.

You are, then, to be not only book readers but bookmakers; though you need not write them. When you talk of reading I do not care to hear your catalogue; I would rather hear you talk awhile. Why? For the same reason that I prefer to have a slice of bread on my plate, rather than

---

* William M. Hunt.

the single ingredients that enter into bread-making. The bread of knowledge, too, I look for in you, not the grains that have been ground to make it. Seeing and thinking by proxy are ruinous to the individuality. Why—is a healthy form of speech when honest inquiry lies at the back of it.

Has it not often occurred to you that gleaning brings more to one than reaping to another? It is keeping what you get that piles up riches. How many of you can tell me how much you can read in a minute or how far you can walk in a minute? I do not ask this because I set any particular value on that kind of inquiry, but I do like that form of accuracy when it is properly directed. Labor of any kind is always suggestive to the laborer; very often its suggestions are of utmost value when exploited. These opportunities to do original work or carry out original investigation are the blossoms of labor; what good comes by continually snapping them off in the bud? None; but a good deal of harm comes. When truth may be made clearer by study, the study becomes a duty. Hence you will take great care of the hints you get from your daily work. If by an hour's reading or an hour's labor a single suggestion of value comes to you what do you lose by letting it go? Do you lose simply the suggestion? No, you lose the hour. Speaking of precious stones Ruskin says : " I question whether after six thousand years of cutting and polishing, there are above two or three people out of any given hundred, who know, or care to know, how a bit of agate or a bit of marble was made or painted." There is plenty of application for that plain statement; one has only to change the factors.

Be readers of good balance; look away from your book frequently. You must plant out of books to reap in them. Do not, in your eagerness to become steeped in knowledge, lose sight of the whole in worrying about a part. Do not be too anxious but work broadly and deeply. Everywhere and at all times you must be yourself. The more you are the shadow of some one else the weaker you are; the less of you there is.

Learn the place of books; know what to do away from them as well as in their presence; if you think only of the latter you miss more than you gain. Be sure that if you can tell me a dozen facts about birds that you have found out for yourself it is better than to read all the books on ornithology and not want to use your eyes. The two labors should go together.

CHAPTER XXII.

LITTLE TOWN LIFE.

Vor when a man do leãve the he'th
An' ruf where vu'st he drew his breath,
Or where he had his bwoyhood's fun,
An' things wer woonce a-zaid an' done
That took his mind, do touch his heart
A little bit, I'll answer vor't.

WILLIAM BARNES.

I would rather you all turned away from this talk and take up that most delightful home book by Mary Russell Mitford—Our Village—than to sit here and listen to me saying awkwardly what I would like to say beautifully. But you are good enough to hear me, I see. What a number of us find everyday life monotonous! We read of distant scenes and places where poets have lived, and all about us dwarfs itself before the bright lands of the imagination We are fond of change, many of us, and buy it dearly. We want to step within the work-a-day world of Burns and Shakespeare; of Schiller and Goethe, of Hugo

233

and Béranger, fancying them to be finer, brighter than all else, but alas; when the hero spirit is absent all such worlds are much alike.

"Our Village" is a delight because it is a surprise the first time you read it, and it is a surprise the first time you read it because it proves to you that the poetry of surroundings has not taken up its abode in one quarter of the world but may be found in the homes and waysides, fields and woods of your own little town as well as elsewhere. You begin at once to think that you too, could write a book about villages, and you might go so far as to try; that certainly would prove that you had at last found out that your village is worth writing about; you would learn to look closely at it, then to love it, and lastly that it is not so easy after all to write books about villages, which might deter you from finishing yours. But that would be no loss perhaps, and the discovered country would be a paradise for you to wander in, and no one knows how much good you might draw from it. When you have learned to pry into the poetry of everyday life there is no village too small to prove an everlasting study; the joy and sweetness it adds to life is beyond the pictures any one may try to draw of it. Do you think your surroundings are mean and common-place? Somebody shall make them famous one of these days, then you may conceive that your common-place opinion comes from a common-place perception. A poet must touch the earth before the rest of us see its beauty. It is the old story of the Sleeping Beauty, the court is drowsy until the prince comes. Washington Irving one day found a poet in Kirk Alloway, he was a carpenter but that need not imply he lacked the poet: " It seems as if the country had grown more beautiful, since Burns has written his bonnie little songs about it," he said.

Can you as artists cultivate too broadly the true love for the beautiful? Is it not good now and then to study the beautiful on which the hand of God has left its mark? Yes, far better as a wholesome, healthful stimulant, to do this than live forever studying lines and angles, curves and arabesques ; these, too, are beautiful but they are not all. There is not one relationship into which you come as a musician that is not in some sense inspiring. Did you ever think that the poets and artists and writers have many of them lived in a little world? Often it has been a mere country village which they so loved that they modestly sung about it, so sweetly that all the world soon learned to love it, too. Who would say, for example, that Dorothy and William Wordsworth did not find enchantment in rural England? They certainly left enchantment upon it and they did not minister it

from a palace either.   It was toward the end of the
last century that this brother and sister left their
house in Alfaxden, resolved to find a settled home.
They chose Grasmere, in the North, and walked
from Wensleydale to Kendal, "accomplishing as
much as twenty miles in a day, over uneven roads
frozen into rocks, in the teeth of a keen wind and
driving snow, and arriving at Grasmere on the
shortest day of the last year of [the] last century,
they took up their abode in the cottage which
may still be seen standing at a little distance from
the main road from Rydal.   It was but a laborer's
cottage but it was all they wanted.   It contained
three low rooms and two garrets under the roof,
but it sheltered them when they were indoors, and
held the books so dear to both.   One of its windows
was a long low one with small diamond panes
through which roses looked in at almost every
season of the year, and there was a small orchard
and still smaller garden rising up behind, with
rocks and a small spring, being in reality a bit of
the mountain which had been captured and enclosed."   These are simple ingredients, are they
not, for the happy surroundings of a poet?   How
many of you live in a place, to say the least, quite
as enchanting as the English Lakes?   It is not
the place so much but the poet within that takes
up the ordinary with his subtle touch, who is led

to look for beauty in every tree and leaf, every lane and by-path. It is curious that we are so slow in learning about the loveliness that is at our very doors; some one must come and point it out. Since David Cox has painted Hereford scenes every one thinks Hereford is full of beauty.

Some one, I think it was John Ruskin, has summed up the every-day *little* life (that is, the every-day life that is not half lived) as the "constancy of small emotions." Many an existence is frittered away in useless worry about little wishes, little sorrows, little doings, little talk, and little gossip; as if life was to be thrown away in any such littleness. Such life is a sin to such as you who are able to solve the problem of living and of existence by dwelling in the delightful world of art. At times you think even this wearisome enough, I doubt not; what would life be to you if it were mere toil for the barest necessities of the body, with no beauty, no bright days in a home pleasantly situated, no joy with friends, no smile of content, no thoughtful feeling for to-day, no hope for to-morrow? Will you compare your own home-scenes with the following, by no means rare cases, of London shop-girls? *

---

* These data were furnished to Dinah Mulock Craik, by two benevolent women, who undertook to alleviate the darkened life-condition of many poor girls and women whose existence is simply a fight with the world for the scanty means they must have to live. I have indicated the earnings in our own money, not in English, as it appears in Mrs. Craik's article.

"A——, Mantle-maker in a large establishment. Wages $2.25 per week, latterly only $1.87, work being slack. Pays 87 cents for room, 25 cents for coal, lamp-oil, and fire-wood, 18 cents for washing, which leaves just 95 cents for food and clothing. Lives mostly on bread and tea; carries bread-and-butter for her dinner to her place of business, as it takes her three hours to walk there and back. A kind forewoman paid for her coming to the House of Rest. She is a pretty, graceful girl of twenty. She said once, with a sigh, ' It is *so* hard to keep respectable !'

"B—— is a bodice hand. After five years' experience earns $2.00 a week. Says simply, ' Often I don't get *quite* enough to eat.' Has no parents; boards with a step-mother. Her sister earns only $1.62 a week. They have hard work to get decent clothes; and the town they live in, a gay watering-place, makes it difficult to keep respectable.

"C—— was a girl, pale and fierce-looking. She had been long out of work with pleurisy and an injured limb. Lives mostly on tea. When quite well (if ever) she rises at 5.30 A.M., and goes to bed at midnight. She too is an orphan, alone in the world.

"D——, a mantle-cutter. Cloth so heavy to lift that she strained her back, result being neuralgia of the spine. She had an invalid sister to support;

and her regular work only lasts through eight months of the year."

Perhaps you wonder what all this has to do with art, why I bring before you, students of one of the most beautiful worlds one can inhabit, this depressing picture of the London poor. There is a reason. Much of the joy of living falls to your lot, so much that many of you are satiated with this pleasure and that; let us suppose for a moment that just the part of life's joy and beauty that you carelessly miss could be given to these poor ones who not only lack the mind-food of life, but the body-food as well; let us suppose that the opportunities, which one by one you let slip by, half-mindful of their value, yet not so mindful that you stop them and turn them to use, let us suppose that instead of running to waste they could be gathered and given to those who have none, what then?

If your little town may teach you to study and to love the beauties of nature with which God has adorned it, if it teaches you that beauty brightens life, may it not teach you to be willing now and then, at least, to tell others about it, admit it to their lives, share with them the abundance that you cannot possibly consume yourself. If art is the truth beautifully expressed it should be more to us than the vantage ground of trade and dicker. If it is no more, how sorry is the sight! I do not think I can feel pleased to know that this young woman, for example, has so many pupils come to her from friends in society that she must labor, busily as a loom, from week to week, so engrossed in making players and money that she is always a loom, and nothing more. Have you ever asked yourself what real good you are doing the world by spending your life in teaching others to perform this air and that, pleasingly ? Really that is all the art of music amounts to with many. I do not see that by so doing one contributes, even very indirectly, to sending a single ray of sunshine into the life of, let us say, a London shop-girl, for example, who, with a pain in her poor heart that is never absent, says simply, " often I don't get *quite* enough to eat." And now may I not say this to you : *If music is only an ornament to you, if you make of it only an ornament for others, you are wasting your life in it.* And to waste a life means what ?

But what about Little Town Life ? It should be the first world to you, where your thoughts can play, where you can see beauty come and go, where you can see the simple home-life of the people where you can see in various intensities the relationship between man and man. Marry it to your art—and you will find the wisdom of the one is the wisdom of the other, the phases here are paralleled there, the same earnestness is manifested and demanded from him who would see much. Just as flippant life in nature keeps one blind to the lesser beauties of the dwelling, so flippant life in art is the outcome of that lack of perception which fails to divine that art is for the noble purpose of being useful, beautiful, and inspiring, all at the same time.

CHAPTER XXIII.

THE INSPIRATION OF THE YEAR.

Winter soon blows your head clear of fog and makes you see things as they are. I thank him for it.

> Spring is strong and virtuous,
> Broad-sowing, cheerful, plenteous,
> Quickening underneath the mould
> Grains beyond the price of gold.
>
> EMERSON (*May-Day*).

What a beautiful gift is a year! All it brings is lovely, and such contrasts! such lights and shades! day and night, flower and snow-flake, summer-breeze and winter-wind, singing brook and moaning sea, brilliant petal and withered grass-blade! To-day the tree-trunk is moss-covered, to-morrow hail and snow pelt against it; a while ago the robin built in the apple-tree, now the blast howls about the empty nest. In every scene in nature there is an opposite; the beautiful seems to have become unbeautiful; but it is not so. The scenes are changed that we may get deeper into them. And nature is such a wonderful, bountiful provider that every minute she puts before us a new theme, brings us a new lesson, never once lets us weary of her doings. Every minute in the hour has its peculiar value, every day its color, every week its distance, every season its aroma. Years are the long days of life; their phases are reflected upon you, move you hither and thither, give you sunshine and shadow, bring you joy and pain. Such a wondrous gallery is the year! with its multitude of pictures, so numerous that we are often blind to their presence! How nature strives to make us wise in her ways—but no, we will not understand her entreaties; yet she is just as patient, just as willing, just as wonderful.

If you would possess the inward satisfaction that assures you of living truly day by day, be a willing, eager learner in the school-room of the year. Artists as you are, you will find the fullest developed art lessons in everything about you. Do not be content to conceive art as something made by men as a recreation to others; it is one element in life, and if you will study the scenes and phases of the years, as they roll on, you will be gratified to know that it is one of the most sublime, yet simple, of life's phases.

You must learn, both as artists and as practical men and women, that we must first realize before we can idealize. If you will become keen observers in the garden of the year, you will gather such a fund of learning in beauty, truth and reason that the new possession will illumine your art beyond conception. Then you will realize, what is a deep truth, which is this: if you miss the teachings of the year, you miss the poetry of life. Be as much the lover of the day and of season as you can; there are such rare scenes in them that touch the heart and make one love the earth which we make our dwelling place. " I would not slight this wondrous world. I love its day and night. Its flowers and fruits are dear to me. I would not willfully lose sight of a departing cloud. Every year opens new beauty in a star; or in a purple gentian fringed with loveliness." * So should you be the dear lover of the year. How many have you lived already? Answer yourself this, then tell us all, in perfect frankness, what so many years have brought you; I do not mean what books you may have read, men you may have known, deeds you may have done, I simply mean what has this wondrous passing show of the year done to make you wiser or better; let me ask what wisdom you have gathered as you wandered onward through the variegated hours of your life? When you bid goodnight to the year's days are they all blanks? There should not be one among them.

You must love the world in which you live or you will not work well in it. There is no half-truth

* Theodore Parker.

in this. What do you mean by raving about the beauties of art? you who have not yet begun to find beauty in leaf-forms, in the curl of petals, in the law of order in parts which is traceable in every blossom; what means it that you are tracing out natural designs in Architectural work when as yet you are not even a student of nature's alphabet? The poets and painters, sculptors and builders win name and fame by crystallizing the events of the years. Every season sends out a rare blossom of a day, does not that mean something? "Do you ever wonder why poets talk so much about flowers? Did you ever hear of a poet who did not talk about them? . . . Look at Nature. She never wearies of saying over her floral pater-noster. In the crevices of Cyclopean walls,—on the mounds that bury huge cities,—in the dust where men lie, dust also,—still that same sweet prayer and benediction. The Amen! of Nature is always a flower."* The more we study nature the closer we come to God. That is another truth with no half-measures about it. I have defined the word—artist—so many times that I am going to do it again,— an artist is one who so loves truth that he cannot keep from putting it in the most beautiful form. We are fond of letting fancy weave an ideal world for the poets

---

* Dr. O. W. Holmes.

and artists whose names and thoughts have come down to us. If you ever wander about the little town of Ayr, in Scotland, you will find there no special beauty that could have forced the poetry from the singer of Scotia. The Bonny Doon is much like other streams, the blue-bell and daisy blossom in many other places. But the mind that can see great truth and beauty in daisies and blue-bells, in little streams and dimly outlined mountains is the enchanting power that tells the secret of all these things. Is the world full of monotony? No, it cannot be, for poets live in it.

We are children, all our lives, in many ways. How eagerly we watch the seasons! To-day it is a sign of spring that sets us all a-talking; very soon the apple-trees are blooming and we wonder how much fruit there shall be; but when the fruit is ready for gathering the leaves are turning, yellow and bronze and scarlet, then they fall, as if they too would follow the fruit, and very soon some one exclaims, excitedly, " I have seen a snowflake!"

And so it goes, every twelvemonth! But do you dread the coming of another spring because it may be like the last? No. No one ever did.

You can get inspiration from the year because there is so much that is remarkable in it. What a rich knowledge you would gather if you were keenly sensitive to all its changes. These beauties of the year should color your thought. As you weave scenes into the cloth of life you must not miss them. Every artist has been deeply moved by the phases of the seasons. Not one of them has escaped the influence of this theme. It is pictured in the mythology of races that have passed away; it will be sung by poets forever.

Spring comes with its broad themes—the flowers and warm rains—but it has rich colorings of many other kinds. The soil is warming; how rich and mild is its color when the plow turns it! Even before the winter has gone the singing brooks have coaxed many a blade of grass to come forth; very soon the violets in the lowland send out their buds; then the trees change and the green that was first seen in the lowland mounts higher and higher. Spring takes a very lowly beginning and moves constantly upward, the birds look up and sing, every flower looks upward to the blue sky, and the blue sky itself seems to have moved farther away, higher than it was before. And what must he do who contemplates all this? Let him do the same—look upward!

You know that nature is beautiful; nature is also wise. In Autumn, go out and study how carefully she provides for her charges. To the maple-seed she gives wings, to the aster and the dandelion a feathery plume, to the balsam a springing pod; the tender buds that are to burst when winter is gone are carefully provided with covering, a scale, perhaps, such she gives to the pear and apple; a woolly covering to the horse-chestnut, an enveloping stem to the sumac; little plants, tiny forests, are stored away in seeds and in quiescent roots. There must be time of rest for all this new life to develop, so the winter season or the rainy months fill up the gap.

Now all these occurrences are very common, you have seen them time and again for years, and may question my right to say aught about such common events. My motive is very simple; I want to hear each of you tell what beauty has come into your life—taught by the beauty of nature in the year? what wisdom have you gathered from nature's wisdom? what poetry have you gathered from your surroundings? If you have learned anything tell us what it is; if, nothing, perhaps this homely talk about everyday happening will make you think. Let us hear! one of you shall speak: Just now I see a meaning in everything. Sometimes the teaching brings truth negatively, but then the weight of it is greater. Life is like a year; it has its seasons and its rare days that sink deep into us. We live through many a changeful epoch but do not know it until the quiet days culminate in a great event. Nature combines more art in a garden plot than one could exhaustively study in the longest twelve-month. Have you not noticed how extensively the artists of building and of decoration use simple means such as the oak leaf and acorn? Try to imagine all the means offered by nature to be similarly employed! It could never be; but we cannot know too much of her beautiful store.

We have talked about the amateur in music, and have seen how good and invaluable he is. Each of you may fill the same place somewhere. Suppose you have a taste for collecting pebbles; you classify them, become sufficiently the amateur lapidary to polish them and give them the best possible setting, arrange them as to order and place and learn the nature of each. Think for a moment what opportunity you would have to gain knowledge by observation even in such a simple way, and the advantage of it would be this,—you would become a keener observer of details in your own field of labor; you would be led to seek relationships and connection in facts—which will be of no harm to you as musicians and which musicians do not, as a rule, think a necessary part of their mental equipment. What about the loiterings in pleasant paths, you may take? They are numerous are they not?

Could you spend a week, any of you, among well-educated strangers, and conceal your professional identity without personal discomfort?

Could you maintain any particular or general conversation so well that your listeners would not think it absolute stupidity in you? I have frequently introduced the subject of flowers and of plant life to you, let me confess for no better reason than because I like them, I delight in studying their ways, forms and colors; but beyond this I deem flower-study of utmost value to an artist for this reason: he finds combined in them perfection in form, beauty in expression, color and light beyond his power to imitate, while besides this they are among the fairest of God's creations. Thus I regard them as the best of surroundings. I wonder how many of you, dwellers in the years, have paid so much heed to these sweet gifts—the smiles of mother-earth—as to have gathered, even passingly interesting knowledge of a few of them that would enable you to tell me:—

1. How many wild flowers you know well?

2. What clime, situation, soil and surrounding does each demand?

8. Of how many of these flowers can you tell the abiding place, from memory?

4. What can you tell of the nature and habits of these flowers?

5. What peculiarities have you noticed in any of them that are not mentioned, so far as you know, by any author?

6. How do these plants propagate?

7. How do they change with the seasons?

8. What personal recollections and impressions have you concerning any of them and what train of thought does the sight of them inspire in you?

9. Are any of them of practical use and if they are in what way?

10. What historic and poetic allusions cluster about them?

11. What are the common and proper names of each; what reason do you know why these names should have been applied?

[In science, names generally mean a great deal.]

These same questions would apply to the trees, which you see every day. Let me imagine that you take a lively interest in trees, so lively that it costs you a genuine pang to see one fall before the axe. Let me further imagine that you know considerable about ten species of trees, that you have one favorite of each, somewhere, about where you live; you watch them from year to year, note their changes with the seasons, rejoice in their first leaves, touch them gently with your hand, love to hear the music of the wind as it passes through them; what a person of interest you would be to meet! I should like to hear you tell of these favorites of yours, watch you as you speak enthusiastically about them, note the warmth in your words and manner. I should approach you with the keenest anticipation, leave you with thanks for having given me so much pleasure, for having taught me that dame Nature smiles because she has a kind heart. Now all that I have said to you of pebbles and flowers and trees you may have thought out for yourself many times; but speaking of them here in our familiar way may make it somewhat clearer to you how much there is in nature that can train the artistic sense, for art is a sense, as you will find out by talking with some one who has it not. You will the more readily comprehend where artists first sought for hints, and what is better still, you will find them there yourself. What your observation has picked up and your thoughts turned over has the mark of your ownership indelibly stamped upon it.

Pictures that you gather in the years of early life impress your surroundings upon the mind with wonderful vividness; if you can only store those early years to the brim and to overflowing with pleasant scenes of your own making and seeking, how much richer your after-inheritance will be! Thus to tune the mind for after years is to provide yourself with untold happiness; even if that happiness be mingled with pain and sorrow it must have lessened them. To create that spirit and to dwell in it in after years, is truly inspiring. The mind, tuned to the truest pleasures in life, will have a sweeter tone than another that continually echoes the discordant NOW.

As you pass onward through the richly laden years, dwell with them; accept what they would give you; gather wisdom which they bring and scatter the same on your own way. The stalactite, formed from the minimum of a water-drop, is a picture of the mind; if the formative matter passes through unclean soil, the hanging is unclean too, if it passes through a purifying soil it is ever the purest white to the very heart.

CHAPTER XXIV.

VACATION TIME AND TRAVEL.

**Wenn jemand eine Rei-e thut,
So kann er was verzählen.**

I felt, what since then has become an acknowledged fact, that traveling would be the best school for me.—HANS CHRISTIAN ANDERSEN.

If you shall chance, Camillo, to visit Bohemia, on the like occasion whereon my services are now on foot, you shall see, as I have said, great difference betwixt our Bohemia and your Sicilia.—*Winter's Tale*, Act I, Scene I.

I can imagine that one of the most delightful books in the world, if some one would only write it, would tell us about the out-door loves of scholars, of their companions in fields and meadows, in garden plots and forests; it would chat to us about all the fascination of the seasons, of the wisdom of nature's ways and the wonderful store of lessons she scatters all about for us. Such a book would teach us that fireside wisdom is not all, even the subleties of metaphysics, deep studies in reasoning, or well-planned arguments do not have in them all the rich and instructive themes that repose everywhere about us.

Music leads very few musicians out of music. I wish it were not so. There is too much else of good and use in the world, that we should spend all our days in any one thing, even so delightful as listening to concord of sweet sounds. I believe earnestly in sailing well out on the sea of life, not in forever skirting its coast, as if we were afraid to drown; yet now and then I would put in at this or that delectable spot, not merely to lie in the sun, though for a moment or two, now and then, I might do that, but to look upon the delicate pink marking of the sea-shells, on the shape and shading of the pebbles, then off to gather flowers and ferns, learn how birds build and where, make a friend here and there among the trees. No matter how far I sailed on the sea of life I would earn my holidays ashore and pass them to my delight, if in no other way than wondering about the strange works that were made by the Hand that created me.

Do you think I should wile away the moments by doing so? Perhaps one now and then, but very few. Even the words of an enthusiast cannot paint to you in too vivid colors the joy of living, if you will study how to live. You must not be unjust to yourselves as musicians by denying your music the salubrious benefit of a near and dear intellectual neighbor. Occupy yourself with one thing forever, it becomes a recluse in your mind, loses its warmth, its fascination; give it a companion and both are happy. Some time, in these talks, I am going to say to you that employment should be easy-fitting, not a yoke to chafe and hang heavily. It should fit comfortably into your existence, so that you are its master, never its slave. When work is thus under your control, you will always make it your duty to do the next task well, so that, when it comes to vacation-time, you will also do its duty well. Know how to work hard and how to rest hard—it sounds homely, but it is worth listening to.

Work is always sweetened by the anticipation of pleasure even if the pleasure lies in a certain variation of the work itself. That is a very healthy sentiment which makes the school-boy whistle merrily when school is done, and the spirit of it is worth keeping through life. One of the best signs of our times is the growing popularity of vacation, for besides affording rest to tired minds and bodies it tells us forcibly that the particular little world we dwell in is not all. Rest days, when we know how to spend them, draw us out of ourselves; scattered through the year they make many bright spots in the little histories that are a constant pleasure to look back upon. Even half-hours spent for change are well invested. In them you learn a little about the garden plot, about the village street, about the village itself and—who knows where to stop? Let me ask you to spend

half an hour some time with Charles Kingsley's
Town Geology, or Ditchfield's English Villages,
Miller's Footprints of the Creator, White's Natural
History of Selbourne, Thoreau's Walden and his
Journals ; they will give you hints as to how you
may use the five senses God has given you. No
poet ever penned truer lines than these—

> " But nature is not solitude :
>   Her many hands reach out to us,
>   Her many tongues are garrulous ;
>   Perpetual riddles of surprise
>   She offers to our ears and eyes."

Little town life and big world life ! one is far the
teacher to the other. How may one speak briefly
of the theory and practice of vacation time ? The
theory is to believe in it, the practice is to have it.

Some of the most exquisite pictures in all literature have been penned by travellers, and, truly,
travel adds not only wisdom to the mind but it puts
pleasing scenes in memory's gallery if only the
traveller loves his art. Some of the most companionable books one can find are books relating the
scenes of wander-years. You now know the story
of Arminius Vambéry, related by himself. Here
is a picture from the book of life, is it not a rich
heritage in the experience of any one ? I quote it
simply for its vividness. The writer travelled in the
East : " As soon as the morning star appears to the

17

eye it is the custom for the whole caravan to hail the coming day. The most zealous person in the company engages in the recital of the Ezan. . .

. . The ablutions are performed in the twilight of the dawn of morning, and before the first rays of the sun touch the crest of the mountains, the caravan stops and morning prayers are engaged in. The animals stand quietly with their heads bent low, whilst the men, with their faces turned toward the East, are kneeling in a line, side by side. . .

. . When the rays of the sun reach the devout faithful, they lift up their voices and chant the melodious prayer beginning with ' God is the Greatest.' " Travel increases the man. " I am a part of all that I have seen." This very thought of incorporating into the self the substance of what transpires before us tells in itself that travel may be made more or less profitable, more or less pleasing, more or less laborious. If it is undertaken with an object that is not too closely akin to the demands of one's everyday life it proves restful, useful and delightful—nothing less. But nowadays travel has become a fashion and people seem to adopt it much for the same reason that they choose this or that style of dress. The world is not to be seen in a day. " You must not think " said Sir Walter Scott to Washington Irving " our neighborhood is to be read in a morning like a newspaper."

Travel is very much like museum study; in truth one may say the world is fast becoming a huge museum through which the travellers race from this curiosity to that. It is a moment in a gallery, another in a famous square, ever seeking out the guide book's tale, instead of using one's eyes and thoughts in making better guide-books than can be had for money. An English writer has very appropriately sketched the traveller whose objective point is nothing : " To come in the morning to a cathedral, to follow the verger through its aisles and chapels, while he tells the story he has told so many hundred times before, and then to take the next train to see the next sight, is to go away knowing as little of it as when you came." *

It is quite wonderful to note the change that has taken place in the way and means of travel. Bayard Taylor's feat in " Views A-foot " is no longer a financial wonder. A view of the world seems denied to scarcely any one, so inexpensive, and comfortable are the means one may command. There is no denying that travel is made an expensive luxury, but it is made so unnecessarily, and any of you who undertake it will find that forethought and common-sense go a long way toward lessening expenses. So to those of you who would see even

---

* Elizabeth Pennell.

a little of the world one may say that not so much is an abundance of money necessary as an abundance of care. One who is so situated in professional music-work that a little can be saved monthly can soon accumulate sufficient means for at least a little wandering. Few have the hardihood to see Europe, a-foot, for two years, with no more than five hundred dollars, and few, perhaps, are satisfied to spend half that amount for fifty days' travel, as Mr. Ballou has planned for those who desire to see much in a short time at a comparatively small cost. The question is not so much how much you can see but how well you can see what you need to see. If you travel even for a short time in the interest of the study you are doing you cannot take too much care in determining what is most especially valuable to you as subject matter for study; see that first and be distracted by the rest after.

Travel brings to one very impressive lessons of places, life, customs and people. The country is of one character, the city of another. "If you would be happy in Berkshire, you must carry mountains in your brain; and if you would enjoy Nahant, you must have an ocean in your soul. Nature plays at dominoes with you; you must match her piece, or she will never give it up to you."* But nature crops out in the towns, too.

---

* Oliver Wendell Holmes.

" In great cities we learn to look the world in the face. We shake hands with stern realities. We see ourselves in others. We become acquainted with the motley, many-sided life of man." *

Nothing is more delightfully anticipated than the first long journey, but the rosy-hued visions of travel are somewhat toned down by the solid hard work that is required to accomplish it. Travel that is undertaken for the sake of gathering at least some special knowledge and general information has its own peculiar difficulties, its common-place, its disagreeable phases ; but also it has all the opposite of these, and all one needs is the rare power of being affected more by the pleasures than the pains. Every traveller should know how to keep a light heart ; how to adapt himself readily to surroundings, even when they are uncomfortable. He should travel with a motive and bring home the fruits of it. He must be as free as possible from encumbrance, and never hurry when it can be avoided. He should know his route before he sets out, and he should make a careful estimate of how he intends to spend his time and his money. Then experience will help him.

In " Les Voyages Amusants " of Chapelle et Bachaumont, the authors say, in the amusing chapter

---

* Longfellow.

that concludes the work : " La passion de voyager est sans contredit la plus digne de l'homme ; elle lui forme l'esprit en lui donnant la pratique de mille choses que la théorie ne saurait démontrer. Je puis en parler aujourd'hui avec connoissance. Il n'y a rien de si sot et de si neuf qu'un Parisien qui n'a jamais sorti des barrières : s'il voit des terres, des près, des bois et des montagnes qui terminent son horizon, il pense que tout cela est inhabitable : il mange du pain et boit du vin à Paris, sans savior comment croissent l'un et l'autre."   One of the most pronounced forms of development in our time is an ever increasing opportunity for avoiding this very provincialism that is so admirably pictured in the chapter from which I have quoted. Travel is good for one, it makes the man more observant, more tolerant, more willing to leave a margin for possibilities in all the comparisons he may draw.   The more one knows of the world the larger it grows, and instead of disorienting one, instead of taking away love for home, it deepens it. " Perhaps no one can thoroughly enjoy his home who does not sometimes travel.   They are like exertion and rest, each the complement of the other ; so that, though it may seem paradoxical, one of the greatest pleasures of travel is the return, and no one who has not travelled can realize the devotion which the wanderer feels for Domiduca, the sweet and gentle goddess who watches over our coming home."* Perhaps you will recall in this connection that touching picture with which Bayard Taylor concludes the recital of his two years' wandering a-foot: "Our homes were not far off. When the twilight grew deeper we parted, and each thought what an experience lay between that moment and the next morning. I took to the fields, plunged into a sea of dewy clover, and made for a light which began to glimmer as it grew darker. When I reached it and looked with the most painful excitement through the window on the unsuspecting group within, there was not one face missing."

Travel is education at first-hand. No worded description can make you feel the immensity of the ocean, the quaintness of another land, the phases of another life. A tour in Europe is the best and most far-reaching lesson in taste-formation that the art student can have; nothing can replace it. But to benefit by it, as by anything else, one must be prepared for it. There are many who are unfit to enjoy the benefits of travel; they get little good from it. As for the university course, the student must have fitted himself previously, to gather the good from it, so in like manner to gather sound fruits from "wander-jahre" as the Germans say, one

---

* Sir John Lubbock.

must be fitted for it, and there is certainly no more delightful study than the spare time, or more, of one or two winters spent in preparing one's self for the university education of travel. With the study thus carried on and the actual observation that supplements it one has a rich heritage of education that could not be had in any other way. Any travel, be it for a long time or for a short time, may be just as carefully prepared by—let me say—preparatory work, and thus it becomes proportionately more valuable. The educated mind is the catholic mind, educated above exclusiveness and egotism. It forms the taste, cultivates observation, and lends a glow to the past that makes retrospect a charm. So it is with a heavy heart that one puts the traveller's staff in the corner at the end of vacation time.

CHAPTER XXV.

LANDMARKS IN LITTLE HISTORIES.

God gives to one man the gift of writing books, speeches or sermons. . . . . . But God bestows on another the gift of living sermons, and wherever the man goes his life preaches. . . . He has his proper gift and he uses it properly. Who shall say he has not turned as many to righteousness as any golden-mouthed Chrysostom of ancient or modern days?—JAMES FREEMAN CLARKE.

Now and then at the book-stores or in the libraries we chance upon a biography, the hero of which is as unknown to us as if he had never been. We think that one who deserves so great an honor as to have his portrait painted at full length for the world, must be one of the heroes of the past, who has in some way succeeded to elude our notice heretofore. So we talk about him with our friends; they tell us assuredly they know nothing of this man; we search for his name in the dictionaries of biography to see how important a place is accorded him, and we find he has not even a mention. After this the volume of biography begins to look forlorn; we begin to regard it in much the same way as we would look at a leaf that is blown about with the other leaves in autumn. Whether or not we sit down determined to find out all the biography can tell, matters little; it is certainly true that this chance meeting with a ghost of the past reminds us how very few of those who have gone before have left a remarkable record—very few I mean, compared with the number of all the company. Then we set to counting on our fingers just how many have impressed our life, and we have not to make the circle of one hand but a few times, which makes us exclaim, "so few out of billions?"

The reduction of a small quantity gives us a very personal hint if we are at all inclined to be self-inclusive in thinking of the passing greatness of mankind. Perhaps we set about weighing our chances, and, if the scales are true, we get but little satisfaction for the trouble. In whichever side we throw ourselves it makes apparently no difference; it seems to say that it matters little to the world in general whether we are in it or out. What of it? Should we be disheartened and lessen the friction of whatever easy-moving, utilitarian life we may be a part of, by suddenly subtracting ourselves from it? Let us look a little farther. There are flowers bright in color, grasses delicate and sweet-scented, leaves of exquisite shape; I can conceive that in a life of bare use and necessity we could get along without all these. But every being is a whit better by their presence; though they neither clothe him nor feed him, still the sight of them is good. So one learns this : if out of many hundreds of billions of ancestors it pleases us to keep fresh in the memory the doing of only a few of them, we pay the many no lack of justice, but these an abundance. How many musicians, think you, are held in the high esteem of studious thought and reverential honor that we pay to a great man? Only a ridiculously small per cent. of them all, which seems to remind us very forcibly of the intensity of that oblivion which is awaiting us, though we feel proud of our exploits.

Now a word for us. We must all believe in little lives, that is the kind we live. It is a healthy and inspiring thought to know that we are, each of us, indispensable. "Whenever we do what we can, we immediately can do more. When men are ascending a mountain, each step, so insignificant in itself, carries them on and up, till new scenes open before them. They have only to keep walking on, taking one step at a time, and presently they find themselves rising above the regions of forests, begin to get glimpses of blue lakes lying below them, of sister peaks rising above them, of the great snow-covered fields which soar upward, pure and cold, into the glittering air ; they see the distant ocean, spotted with white sails, the forest rolling its sea of verdure far away up to the pale horizon. So as we keep doing what we can, steadily, constantly, life opens before us, rich, varied, beautiful, and we find ourselves on great eminences of thought and love, hardly knowing how we came there, for we have been only doing what we could all the time,—no more, no less." *

The music life is much what its lesser lights make it. Their slow but steady on-going gives it health. Music in America is not to be simply the moulding of this leader or of that, but the moulding of all of you. Magnificent beginnings make nothing, it is constant work that tells. No one can afford to sacrifice the bloom of the present moment to uselessness without " a falling off in self-respect." Now the good tone, if I may say it, of a people lies in the preservation of its self-respect. Art, which is the highest development of thought, is nothing without it is less great than he who gave it birth. It is impossible for the art of a people to be beyond its thought; hence, the more a nation is the more it has to put in its literature, its paintings, and its songs. In exactly parallel lines the more you are, the more you have to put in the art you practice; it is great or small with you, useful or useless with you, deep or shallow with you; the parallelism is always perfect.

Some one has said of Coleridge, " he is a man of

---

* James Freeman Clarke.

magnificent beginnings," while some one else (I know not who, in either case), has said what well offsets this : "much of the pleasure of life comes from the sense of getting things finished." With little workers absence of means is often welcomed as an excuse for no activity when a little personal endeavor would readily provide the want. In the particular of supplying his own demand the genius differs from the ordinary individual. The one creates tools to work with if he lacks them, while the other contentedly sits by his block of marble doing nothing, thinking that because he has neither mallet nor chisel he need do nothing. To learn the lesson of increasing means and decreasing wants is a great leap onward toward a success in life ; in art, especially, distinction if it comes at all, comes only for this. Not until the artist has realized the dignity of an artist's office is he eligible to its rewards ; and yet after all, it may be that for his faith he gets little.

Great lives are important because they do everlasting good. Lesser lives are important because they do the good of the day. Each life deserves to be lived to the full, and whichever falls to you is a sacred trust either in its littleness or in its greatness. The heart must be with the treasure be it large or small.

CHAPTER XXVI.

THE FIRST LETTER.

Unpretending mediocrity is good, and genius is glorious; but a weak flavor of genius in an essentially common person is detestable. It spoils the grand neutrality of a commonplace character.—DR. O. W. HOLMES.

[I shall devote this section of our talks to letter reading, to the end that we may study some of the types of individuality that are common enough, to be sure, but which are not studied as they deserve. I intend these letters to serve you a twofold purpose; first, to bring before you personalities for consideration; secondly, to give you some hints in regard to forming an accurate judgment concerning the future of your students. You should set high value on this accuracy of judgment, and yet higher value on the honest expression of it. Some time you may be questioned regarding the advisability of this one or that undertaking art study as a serious employment for life. This is, by no means, a simple matter to decide; I would have you think well upon its seriousness. You owe to your students as much thought, at least, as will make you cognizant with the probable outcome of their art study; less than this is not expected of you.

This letter is addressed to a gentleman, who, late in life, determined to become a professional musician. Items in the personality are as follows: Age, thirty-five; employment, a retail business of small proportion carried on ten miles from a city; education, such as is gained in the grammar and high-schools, supplemented by one year at a business college. Favorite recreation, music at piano together with a little dabbling in composition, carried on in a disorganized way; taste, naturally good, but uncultivated; technic, limited and made very faulty by many years of scrambling, not altogether in its own behalf; character, a surface enthusiasm but little foundation.]

You may believe that I was surprised to read in your letter your determination to become a professional musician. For years you have given your attention, almost wholly to something else so very different that I scarcely know what can have led you to make so radical a change in your life. Your music study has been so limited and so irregular that I can compare it to nothing else than dipping the hand in the waters of the stream on which you are now to embark, knowing nothing as to where it leads you, nothing as to how you should take your course, nothing concerning the way, whether it be pleasant or stormy, broad and easy or narrow and difficult. Have you given these questions any thought? Have you looked well at the position in which you are and in which you would be, that you may know what change must come into every detail of your life before you can be recognized as an artist? Has it occurred to you that all the manipulative skill with which we manage the affairs of after-life is gathered in early years? We are prone, not merely to form habits, but to form them early in life. Especially with such as you this is true, for very little has varied the even monotony of your life. Surely, then, you know, that being midway on the promised life-journey, a determination to take up a new work that shall absorb all your activity is no unmeaning change, and to me it seems all the more remarkable because I know that you do not possess one single qualification fully developed that will be of any assistance to you.

For years, your mind and hands have been engaged in work quite the opposite of any demand of the art life. You have acquired neither the manual nor the mental technic, indispensable

18

to any one who would delve as deeply in art-matters as I know your desire pictures to be your possibility. You tell me that you do not expect to train your hands to expert performance. You can readily see that work and habit have so thoroughly fixed them that it would be a vain wish to train them beyond a very limited degree. It is plain to you that there exists a deficiency in your hands that cannot be overcome. Now you must not forget that as your hands have become characterized by your employment in the channels of business so your mind has acquired a parallel character which will constantly force itself upon you. Your side-study of music has been extremely limited and at no time have I known you to sacrifice anything to gain an hour or two with it, so I am led to look upon this sudden announcement of your determination to become a musician more as a strong surface wish than a well-founded intention that you are certain to carry out.

By expressing willingness to consider technic aside you think to have put out of the way the most stubborn impediment to your wished-for success. You are wrong in that thought. What you will suffer from most of all is the mental starvation which you have been under for many years; too many years, I fear. Your thought has become fixed in the demands made upon it in business.   That condition cannot be easily altered. You must not take it amiss that I thus allude to your mental acquirement; I doubt not you have found it all that was necessary *for what you have been doing*.   But now you are about to become a member of the art-world and in that connection your past mental training is worth scarcely anything. Hence you must make up your mind that all you would be as an artist you have yet to acquire; further than this you are not yet prepared to set about acquiring it.   You tell me frankly in your letter that you are content to remain at the foot of the ladder ; do not forget, even in your willingness, that it will take you some time even to get there. (I do not doubt you feel keenly the pointedness of my remarks; you asked for an honest expression of opinion and you are getting it.)

Before you can do anything of the slightest import in art you must first have had training, plenty of it and of the right sort.   Now it requires time to get training and plenty of time, at that. Any one who begins in youth to obtain a scientific or artistic professional education cannot expect any considerable recognition of his labor within ten years.   It will take that length of time for him to feel at home in his work.   To profit by ten years of study one must pass ten years of unusual activity.   Not the time alone but what is done in it brings the result one hopes for.   In early years both hand and mind learn quickly.   In middle life the untrained members move slowly.   Although in youth enthusiasm and haste frequently spoil a task, it is undeniably true that then is the best time to learn, the best time to store up thought material, the best time to put both mind and body in that fine running order indispensable to living the intellectual life.   You have never yet departed, in but a very little, from the demands of every day existence.   You have in no way fitted yourself to be what you now aspire to.   In every particular you have to live the preparatory period of the young student, a phase with which you should have been perfectly familiar twenty years ago.   Although St. Petersburg is built on a marsh the marsh was first made ready to support the fair city it now bears. In your own case I fear you will never reach the building of the city.   The probable results of your art study are these :—

(*a*) It is doubtful if in less than ten years you could hope to join the intellectual art-world towards which you aspire.

(*b*) During the greater part of that time you would earn nothing, and at the end of it comparatively little.

(*c*) You will have to create for yourself a new world both within and without, which at your time of life is accomplished but slowly.

(*a*) At thirty-five a man is opinionated, more especially, if, as in your case, he has never needed to express opinion. The youthful learner gains the greater part of his knowledge by possessing that elasticity of mind and feeling which recovers rapidly from having opinion laughed at or broken down without ceremony.

(*e*) You are not likely to become a broad-minded artist for the reason that you will accept but slowly the great amount of unexplained instruction you will receive from your teachers.

There is yet another consideration upon which I have not touched, and it will weigh heavily against you. Never having done, as yet, any considerable amount of intellectual labor, you will find it impossible to accomplish considerable study at once. To become a serious student and spend many hours daily at your tasks would so completely revolutionize your life and being that I doubt if you could sustain the strain. It is too unlike anything you have ever done. When you consider that to become a musician, of value to yourself and the art you practice, you must have a wide acquaintance with the many phases of art life in all its generality and with music in all its particulars, with the history and science of instruction, with the best thought of the day ; that you must have seen great works of art, heard the finest music, know the best writers of all times ; that you must have traveled and gathered much by observation, you will then understand that no mere matter of fancy can make you what you desire to be, and further than this, no mere matter of fancy should lead you to try it.

Let me now touch upon that part of your letter in which you speak of the good you may do among learners of art by cultivating taste in them.

All but a limited amount of the opportunity that the average excellent art-teacher exerts comes to him in the way of business. That is to say, his missionary work, if I may so call it, is done in the actual business of his teaching. Now before you can do any good in this way you must first command a public by your generally acknowledged excellence as an artist. You know that this is beyond your possibility for a considerable time. I feel sure in saying that by employing music as an avocation and studying it as I know your opportunity will allow, you can do even more good than by spending a dozen years of your life preparing to work from an acknowledged position, which, by the way, you are not sure of getting. You have now at your command much time that you are at liberty to devote to any side study you may care to follow.

Why, then, is it not best for you to retain your business, which is an assured living, and practice art in a systematic way? Indeed your position in life is enviable in the opportunity you have for doing this. But as I consider it I smile at the old question that has come to my mind so many times, why have you not in the past made systematic study of music, you who have the time for it and avow so much affection for it?

You will say, as you read this, that I have given you not one word of encouragement, and that I have indirectly told you to leave art to artists. What I do mean is this: study music if you will, and as much as you will; but, at this time of life, do not set too dear a hope on a brilliant success as a professional musician. In music as an avocation you will cultivate the beautiful within you ; but in music study as a business you will be exhibiting constantly your unfitness.

I have already hinted at the fact that you would have to make many sacrifices if you begin the serious study of art, and I have also said that, at no time, do I remember you to have made a single little sacrifice to gain an hour or two with it; do you think that now these opposing forces in your nature would reconcile themselves to the disagreeable hard work you would have to perform ? In all the composition you have done I have had constantly to complain of one fault: you finish nothing; but begin a multitude of new works in a little time. I recognize in this more freak of fancy than deep-founded intention. These traits, that have been a part of you so long, are indications—symptoms— of what you will do in all you undertake. If it were not too presumptuous, I could point out to you where you have failed to make a good business better from the same reason that you fail to make finished works of the songs you begin. Your lack of definiteness, of fullness, of earnestness in what you do lies not in the uncongeniality of your task but in you. You are not exacting enough with yourself. You have so long floated comfortably down the stream of life that one can hardly expect you to turn now and manfully fight your way up against the current, gaining every inch in severe struggle; and this is what you must do before you can begin to realize in faintest lines the vision of your possibility. There is a letter by Robert Schumann that would be of value to you; thinking you may not have it I will copy it here for you; it is particularly valuable now because it so accurately fits your case: " Have you the courage to face the long time which will have to elapse before you may *possibly* see your way to a secure position, to bear the thousand deprivations and humiliations without sacrificing your youth and your creative power?

Then, it seems to me your ideas are far beyond your capabilities. You would have much, very much, to make up—a great deal that musicians of your age have done with long ago; and you would have to go through a severe training in any case. . . . . . So I advise you to go on loving art, as you have always done, to keep yourself in practice, and produce things in your mind as much as possible, to follow the lines of our great examples and masters —above all Bach, Mozart and Beethoven—and always give the present a kindly glance. But only after the severest self-examination must you adopt the career to which your heart inclines you, and, if you do not feel strong enough to brave its toils and dangers, seek that safe ground which you can always adorn with the fruits of your own imagination and those of your favorite artists."

I have spoken very plainly in this letter, and you may be prone to judge me in a wrong sense; nevertheless I am confident that I have expressed not a single thought that does not bear directly upon your best interests; the truth of this you will acknowledge when you have pondered upon your own proposed change, as I have. Remember, that while it is a comparatively easy matter to transplant a young tree, an older one is moved only with fatal consequences. I believe, decidedly, in the late learner, for the general reason that I believe in learning ; but in this letter I have not been considering this phase of the question, but the objective point at which you momentarily aim. There is little satisfaction in dwelling upon what might have been, but I will say this: Had you, during all the years of your amateur music life, been a careful learner, a patient inquirer, a studious adviser in art matters, had you proceeded systematically and finished your tasks, you would now be in possession of an admirable preparation for taking your place in the art-world. As it is you have nothing. In closing let me ask you, in all earnestness, to look well about you, behind you, and to the future; look well before you leap, and when you are ready—do not leap.

CHAPTER XXVII.

THE SECOND LETTER.

Beauty no other thing is, than a beam
Flash'd out between the middle and extreme.
—ROBERT HERRICK.

[This letter, from a teacher in a country town, needs no word of introduction.   You will recognize how much truth there is in it and appreciate the difficulty with which an ardent teacher upholds her ideality and honors her ambition in surroundings that are not only restricted but uncongenial. In talking of art, as we have done, no topic could come before us more interesting and worthy of attention than this one.   Those who are fortunately and congenially located in art practice may be given to looking down upon the lowly worker. If there are any such I warn them to pay heed to what they do or they may scorn where they should praise. Instructors are not few who work in a remote corner with more honor to all concerned than many others who fill great places. I commend this letter for its truthfulness and sincerity.]

It was very good of you to write to me for a
letter about my life in Brompton, " in and out of
music" as you express it.   Am I willing to tell
you about my life here in this quiet town?   *Ça va
sans dire.*   I hope the telling of it may not weary
you, as the living of it does me at times ; but I am
cheerful, as you know, trusting that if my life be a
rose it will some day blossom ; yet here the bud
develops slowly.

One need not describe such a town as Brompton.
Besides, you know about it and have noticed that
various manufacturing industries which bring together a few thousand people give a color to a place
if they do not actually make it, and though this
element of our town's population enters but slightly
into my work, I cannot overlook its presence in
speaking in this connection.   Towns are individual,
like people, and are marked by traits of population
—but, as to my own story.

I am quite as busy as ever this year, between
teaching, work at home (about the household) and
the study I try to struggle on with by myself.   Of
my pupils some are bright, some are dull ; all are
interesting in some way but all are not designed
. to learn the music art.   As much as I try to make
clear to them the little beauties of music which I
think lie within their conception the more I am
impressed with the belief that something in nature,

training or surroundings (perhaps in all combined) works against the sense of beauty that I once supposed to be a part of us all.

Art teaching here is unique. Of the dozen pupils I have (I never dare call them by your word, " students ") not one puts any serious hope in anything I may require as a task. Of a child I should not expect seriousness of the nature I mean, but of one who has well-nigh outstripped the teens it is not an expectation beyond reason. I have five such pupils, of both sexes. All of them are allowed by their parents to study music because it is supposed to be a graceful and desirable accomplishment. These parents are of themselves a fruitful source of study. If the child does well, by which I mean, if the child's playing happens to please the father or mother, it is generously praised and exhibited in Brompton drawing rooms. If, on the other hand, the child fails to do this I am importuned to push the pupil forward and " make her play like Mrs. Brown's girl." I do my best to teach each of my pupils as I think the special needs may require, but I confess my plans are often set awry by these fathers and mothers, who, though they listen to my explanations in polite silence, still insist that (as it was put to me by the last remonstrant) " there 's no sense in paying for lessons and getting no music."

So not by argument but by skillful manipulation of rather awkward means do I succeed in working in the good with the ordinary. If it were my fortune to have so much teaching at my command that I could refuse freely this dull one and that stupid one I might, in a short time, gather a congenial class about me. But it is quite otherwise. I *must* get a living. Certain circumstances, of which you know, compel me to live here at home; there is nothing else than music to which I can turn for self-support and—that is the whole story. Every one considers me especially fortunate to have as many pupils as I have succeeded in getting. To-day I am questioned by one dame : "*just* how many lessons do you give a week, Miss Williams?" To-morrow her neighbor remarks incidentally that if she knew "*just* how much I asked" for lessons she might be able to recommend me. A little multiplication with these two factors gives my good friends an idea of my prosperity—I blush to write the word.

Will you tell me what one can do situated as I am ? The necessity that compels me to earn compels me to accept every pupil I can get, talented or dull. Some of them I know, from the first hour, can learn nothing in music. But I know that it is often with them less a dear wish to learn music than a fancied pleasure, so I set to work with a will, and

I honestly avow to you that for every one I do all that is in my power. I reason thus—if circumstances compel me to take pupils of little talent and of none, I must be content to carry the burden, light or heavy, as it may chance to be. Twice I have been compelled to give up a pupil because I could arouse nothing, but it has happened only twice. Now will you tell me if private teachers of any class have any moral right to retain by this or that means pupils whom they know cannot learn what an expectant parent may fancy for them?

Some have used a deft argument—if one insists on spending money in such a fruitless cause I may as well have it as you. But I do not see its justness. In a country town, such as Brompton, it is not music for art's sake, but music for a living. How little I thought, in my days of delightful study, that I should ever be driven into this corner! And the tears I have shed! They only lighted my care for a moment, not forever. Yet, before you condole with me over my misfortune, let me say that even I have interesting hours with my learners. Sometimes I bring them together and play for them, tell them something of interest about music and musicians, guide their faltering footsteps by a walk in any pleasant path which I think may yield them pleasurable gain. When I see that I have aroused an interest I work upon it for all I can get from it;

thus, by strenuous efforts, I gather to them a little fruit and to myself a little satisfaction, as welcome as a draught of water to a parched throat.

As I have said before, a country teacher, like myself, with her flock of indiscriminates, has not only various pupil minds to feed, but more various wishes of parents and friends to satisfy ; people who possess, in most instances, a selective power of questionable nature to say the least.   Desirous as I am to train my flock in the way it should go, I meet many a counter current that considerably alters the little planning I may do.   To-day a good mother comes to me with a piece of music she has chanced to hear somewhere ; she has borrowed it, and wants to know if Millie may not learn it.   By some mysterious chance it is invariably the most unfit thing that Millie could have.   I explain this, and as an offset to my reason I am requested in a tone of docile simplicity that would make your hair stand on end—" Please just let her try it, Miss Williams, and if she can't get it there'll be no harm done."   I can deal with this matter of lack of good taste only by a process of gradual restraint that. may, imperceptibly, change things for the better. To accomplish this, even in a measure, demands more tact than one would think who does not know; so I often teach what I do not admire because I hope it may serve as a stepping stone to something a little higher, and so on upwards, if gravitation downwards is not too strong for me. A short arc of a large circle is not unlike a straight line to the casual glance; give it place to determine itself and it will define its inclination. On this principle of the apparent straight line I must meet the most hopeless taste, praying that patience and time will display to my heart's delight the graceful curve of my line of endeavor.

Dear as art is to me, I know that I must not expect too much, even for its sake, from those in my charge. The highly endowed artist who enchants the cultivated audience before whom he appears, and deigns not to display his ability out of their presence, could not—and certainly would not—do what I have to do. So I content myself by saying that I have a place; I fill it and accomplish some good; only a little to be sure, but yet some good.

I am becoming somewhat positive regarding myself, which you must forgive if it appears too forcible from so humble a personage. If I am the type of a class of teachers, and I think I am, for there is nothing unusual either in myself or in my surroundings, I am certainly of the opinion that we have a place which we can fill with honor to ourselves. If we cannot work in silk, give us coarser fabric, and let us see what we can make of that. But I must say for my part that now and then I do get a bit of silk. When a little child looks up eagerly to me in its desire to be interested do you not think I have an endless pleasure in store? Pardon me the question; I know you can forgive it.

Now I have said enough about my teaching and it is very little, is it not, when it is said? My study I carry on as I can; there are many disadvantages in working alone and at a considerable distance from a city, as I am. I take great delight in the reading I can do; it is inspiring and gives me good thoughts for all my hours. I inclose a list of the last books I have read and will ask you for suggestions as to what might follow; something companionable, if you please, that will instruct me and draw me away from weariness. I do little advance music study, strictly speaking, though I have advanced considerably by constantly reviewing former lessons. Shut up alone with them, they have been driven into me, and I may say that only now do I begin fully to comprehend some of the works I was taught in my student days of a few years ago.

Ever your friend,
CHARLOTTE WILLIAMS.

CHAPTER XXVIII.

THE THIRD LETTER.

It is one of my air castles which I am reducing to solid stone and mortar.
                                        SIR WALTER SCOTT (to Irving).

[To an ambitious Youth who planned more than he could do.]

Your letter is so full of the downright hard-work principle that I am much inclined to laugh at you for writing it, even before I say a word to commend your ambition. Seeking the cause for so abundant an output of promise to do work I should think to find it in this : You have already won some success in your chosen work, you possess a deep love for what you are doing as an artist, you are filled with gratification even in the tasks you perform. These and other reasons have led you to promise yourself so much work for another year that your ambition has run away with your common-sense. The art-life lies before you so full of beauty and of promise, so inviting and so charming, that you cannot be contented with little results. You will see the great world at once, pry into its nooks and corners, seek the joy and the use of wisdom in all that transpires before you. Who can wonder that you are ambitious?   If you were not so one would say you were unworthy of the high office to which you aspire.   But there is much to be said of ambition.   It is an excellent motive power, *when it is controlled*, just as steam or electricity ; but when the force becomes too great the body that it works upon must yield to the pressure.

In the plan of work for the year which you have sent me there is outlined, actually, an alarming amount to do.   You do not comprehend what it implies to sign such a promise as you make in your letter to me.   The daily task you allot yourself must, to be well done, find you mentally and physically at your best every day in the year. You do not seem to admit it as a possibility that your plan may be interfered with by this person and that ; you are now assuming professional life, bear in mind, and you are in consequence public property to the extent of your appeal to the public.   In its construction the plan is admirable, time economy and the industry principle are strong features.   Let us look at it :—

6.30–7. Breakfast.
7–8. German or Italian.
8–11. Instrumental Practice.
11–12. Writing (Music).
12–1. Lunch.
1–4. Teaching.

4–5. Study at Library or Art Museum.

5–6. Dinner.

6–7. Writing (Correspondence, and the like).

7–10. Reading or Concert.

10–6.30. Sleep.

This is exactly as I find it in your letter. Let me now take the liberty to tell you what I think of it, perhaps to suggest a change here and there, hoping thereby you may the better understand your own project. As it is, you have arranged your labor so as to get :—

8½ hours sleep.

13 " work.

2½ " for eating, etc.

0 " for rest during the day.

and very often you sit with book and paper at your elbow during meal times. The regularity with which you promise to shift from one to another topic of your work has in every trait the appearance of the modern railway switch; you do not seem to consider that you are a human being of nerves, muscles, feelings and hopes. Even iron and steel wear rapidly away by moving in the groove they are fitted to.

You are led to heap the work upon yourself now because you think youth the best time to till. You must not expect to become all in a moment as perfect as the models you have before you. Do you remember in the Table Talk of Martin Luther, the reformer's words to an aspiring preacher ?—" You wish to have the harvest and not the first fruits."—It is likewise so with you I fear.

We have a trite expression that is very wise—to lay by something for a rainy day—which has no particular claim to reference to our finances alone. In all youthful resolutions there is too commonly overlooked this : that it is quite as wise an investment to be saving of force as to be saving of money.   I feel it a duty to say that in your plan, logical as it is, you are promising to spend too much power.   You will be able to put aside nothing for the morrow and you certainly will need it if you keep on as you have begun.   Thirteen hours a day is too much work-time for an intellectual man, if it is to be long continued.   In youth, while the man is yet forming, it is even more dangerous than in later life when one may work on the strength of maturity, provided the power has not already been lost by an unwise youth-practice.   An English author,* in an excellent article on " Men and Women," has written some very sensible words about the education of women that are equally applicable to all.   Concerning overwork he says :—

---

* George Romanes.

" For my own part, I believe that, with reasonable precautions against over-pressure, and with due provision for bodily exercise, the higher education of women would *ipso facto* silence the voice of medical opposition. But I am equally persuaded that this can never be the case until it becomes a matter of general recognition among those to whom such education is entrusted, that no girl should ever be allowed to work more than eight hours a day as a *maximum;* that even this will in a large proportional number of cases be found to prove excessive; that without abundant exercise higher education should never be attempted; and that, as a girl is more liable than a boy to insidiously undermine her constitution, every girl who aspires to any distinction in the way of learning should be warned to be constantly on the watch for the earliest symptoms of impairment."

The author was thus led to express himself because a correspondent had drawn for him in one of her letters a picture of the pernicious necessity —if I may so express myself—of doing an immense amount of university work in one day. It is just what you are doing. Here is the quotation, perhaps it will touch a chord responsive in you :—

" I never begin work later than six o'clock, and never work less than ten or eleven hours a day. But within a fortnight or so of my examinations I work fifteen or sixteen hours. Most girls, however, stop at fourteen or fifteen hours, but some of them go on to eighteen hours. Of course, according to the school time-tables, none of us should work more than eight hours; but it is quite impossible for any one to get through the work in that time. For instance, in the time-tables ten minutes is put down for botany, whereas it takes the quickest girl an hour and a half to answer the questions set by the school lecturer."

It is inconceivable how men and women in the growing period of life can endure such strain. If it is true that some of them do continue it without any immediately fatal result, it is equally true that many of them do not. At the same time let us not forget the one truth in labor that places all rules regarding it in a relative attitude. It is this, an amount of work that is burdensome to one is the easy accomplishment of another, admitting good health to be a common factor.

There is another excellent feature about your plan—the work changes; that of itself gives rest. The mind is ever grateful for a change of employment; the variety fertilizes it. By dividing the strain the mind becomes less fatigued. Sustaining power is greater when weight is equally disposed over the entire surface. Yet, notwithstanding the excellencies of your plan, which accounts for every minute as faithfully as that scheme which Franklin shows us in his autobiography, it sorely needs *weeding*. Let me arrange your plan—I may do it badly as far as your wants are concerned, for I shall aim not only at them but at another advantage, as you will see. Here is my arrangement :—

7–7.30. Breakfast.
7.30–8. Free or at Instrumental work—as desirable.
8–10. Instrumental Practice.
11–12. Language Study or Reading.
12–1.30 (2). Lunch.
2–5. Teaching.
5–7. Dinner.
7–10. Free.
10–7. Sleep.

I have lessened your hours of labor because I know you can do more thereby. You can accomplish more professional work, because you will put as much effort in less time as you have previously spread out over a longer period, and you will accomplish more in your avocations, because you will have more hours for them. All of this you will not know until you try it. Your plan makes me think of a man in a straight jacket; as it ought to be you should have all the freedom of an easy fitting coat. Let the mind seek its own rest now and then; nature is very kind in giving warnings and even repeats them.   Meet her wisdom with all you possess.   Have you noticed that approaching weariness makes the mind inactive, so that it loiters about its task as a lazy boy on his way to school?

There is exquisite comfort in knowing that work is done and that an hour for rest has come, but it requires much skill gained from practice to drop the task when rest-time comes.   Time economy and industry are perfected only when we have learned to enjoy in every hour the work or rest assigned to it.   In all labor nothing is so thoroughly comfortable as *room enough*, by which I mean, of course, time enough.   If there is restraint from over-loading, freedom is lost; if there is inactivity from too little, vigor is lost; so it is bad both ways.   In this particular the mind is like a watch, if you persist in winding it one turn too much you make it for a time useless, if you do not wind it sufficiently it fails to keep pace with the day.

It has always been your failing as a student to promise yourself too much, and I see the failing is following you in professional life.   Try to lose your tendency to hurry—it spoils the performance of a musical work, and it will ultimately spoil all you do unless you restrain it.   Plan for the coming year, by all means—every one gains by

planning—but leave a margin for unexpected occurrences, you will need it. I have nothing to say
about your choice of tasks; the work you outline
is dictated to you by necessity and therefore admits
of no change at present.

CHAPTER XXIX.

THE FOURTH LETTER.

A man who has no artistic culture, however superior he may be in other respects, lacks an instrument which is indispensable to his complete use of life.
ERNEST CHESNEAU.

[About a talented child in pernicious surroundings.]

It is quite impossible for me to speak as I should like about the child you have observed so carefully. I only regret that your effort to draw it away from the influences that are working against it has not succeeded. You take a more pessimistic view of the matter, however, than I, which is to be expected, as you have seen the actuality of the case and I only a word-picture of it. Yet my lack of observation in this particular instance gives me one advantage; I can speak to you in a non-partisan manner about the probable force of such early association as your little friend is subjected to. If you can extract a grain of consolation or advice from the little I have to say I shall be pleased.

There is no denial entertained against the fact that early surroundings sink remarkably deep into the nature. In every autobiography this fact is always strikingly brought forth. The hopes and fears of childhood are a sacred theme with autobiographers; and as deep an impression is made upon the child by the people of his early world. How they behaved towards him, whether they repulsed or encouraged his first wishes to do something, whether they spoke a kind or a cruel word, all this and much more works so forcibly upon the young recipient that it remains one of the strongest and foremost factors in life. Now in the consideration of the influence of early life upon any one whose life we may trace backwards, we are prone, first of all, to note how the strength of character combatted its enemy forces and how it made a way for itself when none seemed open. It is difficult to study a life when it is offered to us in portions each a day long. To see its strong characteristics, its lights and shades, its outline and direction, one must look back upon it, the same as with the mountain chain. To study too closely the detail we lose to sight the effect of the whole. Trivial incidents and insufficient evidence of the strength of character are often mistaken for the deeper traits, and thus many wrong estimates of future worth are deduced from absolutely nothing. It is so easy to regard a child as " nothing but a little one," therefore requiring slight consideration. Many parents, friends and guardians ruin the future man or woman for no other reason than ignorance or prejudice, when it is not both. The parents of the child whose interests you champion are committing this blunder, or, may I not say with equal justness and propriety, this crime? With very little opportunity to develop the wonderful amount of talent you have discovered in the child, with no desirable home influences and little hope of bettering the condition, you have, I grant, a disheartening outlook, but such conditions have many a time arrayed themselves against one of us and many a time have the conditions been worsted. Your knowledge of mankind in history will surely convince you as to the truth of this.

Throughout your letter you have failed even to hint at the very piece of information that I regard more potent than all the rest, more potent than talent and surroundings—namely, the individual character of the child, and there is not a child who does not display in one way or another just as much individuality as his elders. Have you observed this talented child in any situation where he has been called upon to act on his independent force of will and character? If you have you should have a key to the whole situation. I admit it is exasperating to have the father laugh carelessly at your earnest words concerning his child's ability; from what I know of him I should expect nothing more. I feel confident that he will, as early as possible, condemn the young boy, to money-earning; that will be a sad event, but I cannot say positively, with you, that it will be the intellectual ruin of the child, morally and mentally; it may be that such a step would be one toward forcing him to start up for himself, one that will force him to act against the power that takes him where he should not go. Remember that many a noble struggle is carried on in childhood.

You want to know my opinion as to whether you should take the boy in your own care until you see him so intellectually formed as to be practically safe for the life you think him best fitted for. This, of course, you have not yet broached to any one else I hope. You must not forget that, unfit as the parents of your little friend may be as guardians of a talented child, they have for it a father's and mother's love as deep and true as may be found. Besides this, these people are of independent spirit and consider themselves—and rightly they should— quite able to look out for their own affairs. You cannot charge these people with a lack of thought but with the lack of a certain kind of thought. They have before them a future for their son as full of richness as you paint, but they do not see but what a way will come to them for realizing it. To be perfectly frank, I think you have shown yourself a trifle too enthusiastic before them. You must remember that the world of letters and of art-beauty which you tell them of and which you open to them is something so new that they fail to realize how you got it or what you may do with it. They do not know how you came into possession of your knowledge; in a word, you have been talking to them from a height and they did not see you.

If nature has designed the child to become an artist there exist there forces for the consummation thereof. A little battling is good; it brings out force; shows the sterner qualities. Look at the combinations in the case. The child is poor and talented and the child must become a man. Let us suppose :—

(*a*) That you relieve the poverty and cultivate the talent; if a strong and noble character develops with the education a man of worth will result; in that case you will have raised a remarkable person from an ordinary level.

(*b*) But if after relieving the want and supplying instruction you find no innate strength and value of character—you will then not only have no artist forthcoming, but you may have ruined a commonplace character by giving it too much decoration in the vain hope of making something better of it. These chances are worth consideration.

Cease for a while to think of probabilities and study carefully the leading traits of character in the

child and in other children as well; is he determined, serious, straightforward, willing ; or are other
traits his ? When the personality of the boy is
clear to you, think how it will fit the art-life and the
art-education. Do not judge on lines too narrow.
From twelve to twenty much change may take place.
The undesirable way of the boy may be lost when
man's estate is reached. With every new experience the character is changed; how changed is
the question. The course for you to pursue seems
logically to suggest itself. Advise him and guide
him as much as you can as he develops from the
home ; it may be against him in some respects, but
decidedly is it for him in others. Help him always
to help himself; if there is anything within it will
make its way forth. Tendencies change with time
even when they are fortified with ability. If a
practical test of your opinion be made, and the result warrants you lending the helpful hand, by all
means do not refuse it. You must not forget that
the home condition of this boy will demand very
soon that he contributes his share to the common
sustenance ; before you unfit him for this be reasonably certain of the steps you are taking. Philanthropy must no go about blindfolded.

I feel certain you will not make the error that
many educationalists blunder upon, and base all
hope for a successful life upon the development of

20

one evidence of ability. Before all things you must consider the man in this child; he must be successful in this first; only afterwards should you give consideration to what he may be as an artist. It is not an uncommon happening, for a person possessing the education you have, to become deeply impressed by the probable future of a child; some successes in life are to be traced to such interest, but always it is the forcible character of the subject that is the strongest factor. In the interest you manifest in this case you must always be perfectly certain whether you are fitting for a higher place or unfitting for a lower. It is with children as with men—with little education some bring forth much, and with much education others bring forth nothing. In a sense, a child of talent born to poor estate must always be superior to his home surroundings if he is to go upward, because it is that superiority and nothing else that wins in the end. And let me say one word further—this superiority must be possessed of every one, no matter what may be the estate, who determines to develop to fullness a rich talent. Do you recall the boyhood of Giovanni Dupré? No matter what condition held him down, he went on going up, because the spirit *of going up* was in him. That spirit must be the handmaid of Talent, and without it Talent is a poverty.

Assuredly then I would let this boy make his own way; stand by and give a hint, a word, a helping hand when such are imperatively needed; you cannot supply the deficiency of determination. If determination is in him it will come out in the little battles he has to fight; hence for some reasons I do not think it for the worst that you are not able to put everything ready done in the hands of the child. It is earning the privilege to live that gives us joy in living. Do not think me advising you against well doing; you should know that I would not do that. You do not know, perhaps, how very much you can do for another, in a word or two, in a little help given at the right time. It is this you should give; valuable experience, however, must come of itself.

Perhaps I can put your own interest before you in a better light by telling you of a child of ability that lives here, near me—a girl of about twelve years, remarkably quick to learn, she has picked up somewhere a sufficient knowledge of piano playing to play simple pieces well, always from memory, and usually without having seen the music, which, by the way, she reads with much ease and commendable correctness; if she is asked to play or to recite (which she does well) before an audience of friends she does so with no hesitation whatever. She shows the same precocity in her study at school, is naturally liked by her little companions and generally noticed by her elders.

This is a very bright picture is it not? But there is more to it. This child is the daughter of a father and mother who are not only uneducated but thoughtless. The child has really brought the parents to notice and they are not only proud of the little one's ability, but foolishly proud of it. While they are pleased in the talent of their child they do not honor it; they carry on their domestic warfare in its presence and keep constantly before it a villainous example in word and action. To a certain extent the child has been allowed a freedom of speech and of action that has robbed it of a child's naïve simplicity and makes it pose as one unseemingly free in all it does. Its confidence has become consciousness and its ability smartness.

This is the saddest of misfortunes, but what can one do against it; one cannot say to these people that they are unfit examples for their own child; nor can one say to them that the child would be better off in other care; such a change is possible only when coming from the voluntary action of the parents. Between the poor man who is unwisely proud of his child's talent but who does not comprehend it, and another who knows how to honor it, there is a vast difference; for if the child must live at home the strongest controlling power is not always its talent but the calibre of the father and mother. To those upon whom it falls as a duty to teach such a child as I have in mind there is possible an excellent opportunity of planting the seeds of good, only hoping that they may be strong enough in their young growth to survive this or that evil influence. When the home does not supply all there is needed, outside influence of teachers in school and in private instruction must do all that can be done to repress the undesirable and bring out strongly those points of character that will develop a man or woman of worth.

CHAPTER XXX.

THE FIFTH LETTER.

[To a young woman whose reputation was ever just ahead of her ability].

[I have ever had a purpose before me in all of these talks. I have endeavored to give you in each of them at least one serviceable thought for which you might find a practical application in your every-day life. I have kept it constantly before me that "the smallest actual good is better than the most magnificent promises of impossibilities.* If I have repeated a thought here and there—and I know that I have—it has been to a purpose; the only way to get a nail into a plank is to drive it there; a homely comparison but forcible, you will admit. The object I have in presenting this letter to you is this—it is always best to have a reserve. Estimates are often grossly unjust and they err in granting too much quite as often as in granting too

---

* Edward Dowden.

little. There is much harm that may come from hearing about one's self. Now and then there comes to our notice some one who has fallen victim to the over-generous praise of friends or public, perhaps of both; then all at once we hear no more and are left to wonder for a day about the once favored one. The light of many a career goes out very mysteriously. When there is little reliance on absolute merit and much faith in the empty words of an undiscriminating talker, only a failure follows. As you study the personality in the letter I read, you will be impressed with the fact that the character instead of being rare is one of the most common.]

Your letter, and the clipping enclosed, gave me much pleasure besides furnishing me with a theme or two for meditation. I have delayed a reply for a good reason; yours is one of those letters that I want to answer when I feel like it; and first I must have had some thought about the matter. Having satisfied myself on both these points, I am now ready for a letter chat with you.

It was very good of your friend to write such warm words of praise about you and your work. I have thought of his words and his interest in you, and I feel free to say that he shows as much sincerity in what he writes as one could; yet there is one thing I do not understand, namely, why he should commit his generous opinion to the publicity of print? He does you honor thereby, I admit, but I doubt if he does you justice. You did not expect this from me, perhaps. No matter, you know that I shall be as honest as one can, so let that suffice. I said your friend does not grant you justice; I will explain what I mean. You are now scarcely twenty-four years of age; your actual professional life as a musician extends not over four years, the first two of which count for little and the other two not much as yet. The clipping which lies before me does not tell us much concerning even the little you have done, but deals rather in what you may be expected to accomplish. I think your friend is right in saying that as a violinist you are destined to receive, as you go on, much recognition for the ability you may develop; I also think it true that you will win praise for your composition, as indeed you have already. But I have one advantage over your friend; while he writes enthusiastically about your present, I have clearly before me your past as well. Being a firm believer in that law of the French writer, Buffon, which says: " Pour juger de ce qui est arrivé, et même de ce qui arrivera, nous n'avons qu'à examiner ce qui arrive," I hold your future accountable to your present and your present to the past.   Now it is not more than four or five years ago that you were written of for the first time by another indulgent friend, who brought into forcible prominence what you *might be expected* to accomplish. Such notices acquire inaccuracy as they travel, and you know as well as I, that you have frequently been credited with the actuality of these predictions without having realized them.

Even in so short a space of time as four years considerable reputation may gather about a musician who has, in a measure, stepped out of his school. This reputation has come to you, but unfortunately you have been continually getting more than you deserve. I can easily account for it—you are in truth a person of talent, you have had excellent educational advantages and have always possessed many influential friends. Of these friends I want to say one word: they have made more reputation for you than your talent and education combined. That is a very plain truth, is it not? Do not misunderstand it; there is more in it than you think. Through the very kindness they have extended to you, they have in a measure made you ; it has ever been your gracious custom to let your artistic ability contribute as much as possible to the pleasure of others ; as a consequence, a thousand kind words and warm praises have been showered upon you. But you must not forget that this happening imposes a duty upon you, which is this, that you be not unduly influenced by what you hear regarding yourself. Never let opinions from this one and that influence you ; those who have the deepest interest will say the least and never flatter you. Count me as one of these, though, just here, I take the liberty for once, of saying a good deal.

Perhaps few turn art so readily into a living as you ; how helpful it is, you will not conceive unless you lose the kind offices of the host of friends who surround you, and I hope this may not happen ; at the same time, will you let me give you one warning word? Keep your future in your own hands ; do not let others have all the making of it. Art is not merely a passport to social and financial success. If art is your life you should have a just appreciation of it. For many reasons it is decidedly unwise and unsafe to leave this kind of account in the hands of others. Once you assume a public place you should be capable of more than filling it. You should have a reserve power. It is concerning this very matter that you have been careless. Your reputation has raced onward so speedily since you came to notice that it has severely taxed you even to endeavor to keep abreast of it. That is not as it should be. Let the reputation be what it will, you should be, always, ahead of it. This seeking to get into notice in trifling ways, the anxiety about little items in success, must not for one moment stand in the way of a clear comprehension of what you are doing as a worker.   Labor steadily onward, never mind approbation; it frequently comes not at all or in the wrong place.   What is lightly earned is not highly prized.   You will find that, in the end, not what your friends say about you but what you really are is the measure of judgment that will be applied to you.

You know a few people in music whose only care is to be more than they are.   They are oftentimes successful, but it is a sorry race they run which one day must come to an inglorious end.   What is the good, let me ask you, of assumption?   It is more difficult to carry on than hard work of an honest kind, and has the undesirable quality of casting an unfavorable aspect on the little real ability one may possess.   Success that accumulates slowly, that accumulates when you know it not, is more dearly bought than success of the day.   One of the best things to know of a young artist is that he works faithfully, and that people know little about him.   In time such a youth will be heard from, or ought to be.

When art is the life-work, as it is with you, all of yourself must be concerned in it.   "All art worthy the name is the energy—neither of the human body alone, nor of the human soul alone, but of both united, one guiding the other; good craftsmanship and work of the fingers, joined with good emotion and work of the heart." You cannot afford to be the plaything of the public, nor to build too deeply on what this variable quantity has to say of you. These flattering opinions that creep into print from time to time may not be amiss, but they must not get in the way. Of all the people who say such good words of you how many do you know to be capable judges of what you are doing? And if they are not in every sense capable judges, what is the use of setting much store by what they say? You must receive compliments graciously and forget them at once, but keep at your work. Industry is the shaping tool.

I have spoken very plainly. Why? Because, like the writer of this clipping beside me, I recognize your ability; but further than this, I see that you are becoming a trifle over-anxious in the race. Never put yourself in a place to have more said of you than you deserve. Your reputation should grow slowly and come from merit; not quickly and spring out of the vagaries of this one and that. I see no content in probable success. There is a constant onward tendency about a life that is earnestly busy which, in a way, makes success as it

goes on just as the mill grinds while there is water.
But when it stops the mill yields nothing. You cannot be too thankful to your friends for good words,
but you can, with the exercise of common sense
graciously applied, judge between the words that
are honest and those which are meant to please.

CHAPTER XXXI.

A FAITHFUL FAILURE.

Life is a leaf of paper white
Whereon each one of us may write
His word or two, and then comes night.

Gently begin! though thou have time
But for a line, be that sublime,—
Not failure, but low aim, is crime.

JAMES RUSSELL LOWELL.

The greatest part of all that is noble and useful in the world lies in the hands of men and women whose names we can never know. The leaders are known, but the army has no name. Earnestness, like real grief, is never clamorous. Who works in obscurity learns to love work and to do it well for its own sake. In nothing more than in art is there needed these workers who are willing to labor faithfully for the sake of the task. I do not say this because I wish any of you purposely to slip away into obscurity; that comes easily enough of itself; my meaning is this, only a vigorous plant can bear a beautiful and vigorous blossom ; the body of the art plant is you ; all of you who by your influence exert power over a limited public are makers of the art public. As you prepare, others may lead. Not all the power lies in the hands of the genius. He must be helped; people must be taught concerning his work and tendency, they must be taught to hear him and give him welcome. It is you who shall do this. I say this freely because I know the genius to be a comparatively rare personality and the chances are I am not talking to one. As St. Bonaventura said of the religious man, so one may say of you : " The best perfection is to do common things in a perfect manner. A constant fidelity in small things is a great and heroic virtue " In the vain chase many of us carry on in the hope of winning a little fame, we lose to sight the real end of living. Assuredly, if you are not of remarkable talent and will be a worker in the art world, you must leave great places to others and be contented with obscurity. Now, having by severe labor found a place in art, and that place an obscure one, what are you going to do there ? I think it would be infinitely better for all of you if you could know with absolute certainty that you and renown could have nothing to do with one another ; then you would be less likely to waste your precious time in worrying about it.

Many a little life is ruined by the dissatisfaction that is brought into it. All of us find out one day, however, that life is a great gift and we would better bestir ourselves and do some good with our existence. Perhaps you think art to be something very fine, superior to mere common employments; so it may be in some ways, but they all meet on a common level when we regard them from certain points of view.

What is art to you? I ask.

The employment I like most and which yields me a living, you say.

Well, here is some one dressed not quite as finely as you, with hands rougher and carriage a trifle awkward, and I say to him :—

What is farming to you?

The employment I like most and which yields me a living.

Very good, now tell me, which of you has the best of it thus far? Now, I am not comparing the one personality with the other to bring to notice any invidious difference, but to show that it is less what a man does but how he does it that stamps a value upon him. ¡The measure of a man's real character, it has been said, is what he would do if he knew it would never be found out. | And it is not until a nation may boast the possession of a host of honest art educators who care nothing whatever

21

about fame that its art soil will prove at all productive. So I should rather know that you slip away into, may I say, active obscurity, than to hear much noise about you for a day or two then—silence forever. The genuine," says Herman Grimm, "finds its way; let a coppered gold-piece and a gilded copper have currency for a while and they will by degrees change their character without anybody's troubling himself to rub or scrub them." Disguise it as you can, value is not altered; it is merely changed in appearance, a little matter which rights itself in time. Once you begin to move, every step carries you somewhere. Whither? you would better be asking yourselves. These steps may not be taken twice; we could right a great many matters if they could. "The retrospect of life swarms with lost opportunities."

You are not to complain that you suffer from limitations. Every human being is so afflicted. Invest wisely the little capital at your command and make the most out of it, and do not mind the comments of those who do nothing but comment. "When an inexperienced person discourages you by not liking your work, ask yourself how many dollars you would give for his opinion." * Look about yourself and discover there are advantages

---

* William Hunt—" Talks About Art."

for you to be doing. The disadvantage is within. "I understood very well how to torment myself," writes Hans Christian Andersen, of his youth, which was by no means a rosy time. By keeping close to his purpose he accomplished something; but such a struggle !

What is commonly dismissed, for convenience, as an ordinary life, may not be ordinary in any sense. You do not know how great a circle the pebble may make until you have dropped it in the water. Even the artist that never wins fame must move onward. If the next century brings forth a greater leader than we acknowledge to-day, the rank and file of the artists will be proportionately better. In awarding the laurel of fame Time is an unscrupulous sifter ; but the fact that you must slip through the meshes is no business of yours just now. Later on that will settle itself.

In the great school-room of Art in America there are many workers and many idlers. The drones manage to live for awhile, but they are eventually thrust out of the way. Among all the serious ones there may be a genius or two ; they are rare, that is why I set my estimate low. All the others make up the body of our art population; they carry the light. Each becomes identified with a certain locality, forms its taste and attitude toward art and artists, is its preceptor and shows that art is not an aristocracy but a beautiful possession for every one who has a warm place for truth and beauty in his heart. This influence that the art educator has upon the public mind is a considerable power, and in the situation that grants it he finds the best possible outlet for well-directed activity. So, very assuredly one sees in art a place for you of little talent, comparatively speaking, but of much earnest industry; there can never be too many of you.

" With the oldest Greeks, the good hymns of the singer, invoking deity, were equal to the offering itself." There is nothing done in earnestness that fails to take root. If your failure to win fame is bought at the expense of everything, if you have simply raced after it and failed to grasp it, where are you as a life worker? If, however, you have not had time to think of fame because you have been actively minding your business, one may congratulate you.

CHAPTER XXXII.

THE BUILDERS.

No history is so full of suggestive scenes and logical action as the history of Architecture. There is fascination in following the development of the art and science of construction. One learns that men have always turned to the means about them, have wrought in it, made for themselves tools to work the wood, the metal, or the stone. The material is soft, and the tools are made well enough to work it; if the material be hard as the porphyry of Egypt, the tool must have the keenest edge, the utmost durability. Because the sycamore and acacia grew abundantly in the valley of the Nile, we find throughout the early art history of this people that it was of these woods they made their statues and statuettes. They worked in wood with more freedom than in stone because it yielded more readily to the action of the hand, and because it was soft and yielded easily they made nothing of it that was intended to last. When the Egyptian builded

325

for eternity he used the hardest stone.   He worked for all time and did his best to leave an honorable record of himself.   Because this or that part of his work might not be seen did not lead him to do it hurriedly.   Even when he built out of sight he built the best he knew how.   "The tomb of the great Seti I, with its passages and chambers, extends for one hundred and forty-five meters into the mountains, . . . and the tomb of Rameses III has a length of one hundred and twenty-five meters. All this vast expanse of wall, ceiling and pillars, except the chambers of sepulture, is carved throughout with the creation of the chisel, to which the painter's brush has given an additional charm.   In one of the largest tombs the excavated surfaces have an area of twenty-three thousand square feet. As no ray of sun penetrates these passages, all this work must have been executed by torchlight; and yet, although the sculptors knew that the entrance to these abodes of the mummy would be permanently concealed, and, if possible, even obliterated, they finished their decorations with the utmost care."*

There is such a complete absence of any desire on the part of the worker to glorify himself in this monstrous labor that he wins our admiration at

*L. M. Mitchell—"History of Ancient Sculpture."   Ch. 3.

once.   Here there is no vain striving to gain momentary fame, still less to win everlasting praise; it is simply a picture of work done for the sake of fulfilling the purpose of the work.   So many of us lose our way in these days of fame-seeking that I hold it to be worth your while to regard long spaces of time as only relatively long and the work of each of us as only relatively important.   The world considers but few of us entitled to a long obituary notice, yet every one may fill a place of much importance if he will but make it so, doing his work for the sake of carrying out, in the best way possible, the demands of the place he is in. Your first composition is great to your own eyes, but it will recede even in your opinion.   We are constantly looking back on yesterday's dwarf of the self, then we say with a feeling of relief that every affair of the moment is strangely too great and distorted in our own eyes.   Do you know that optical illusion known as anamorphosis?   Nine-tenths of what you do to-day will look that way to-morrow if you work much for the glory of the hour.   Perhaps you recall what the French author, Marmontel, says of himself:—

" Who knew better than I that of my first essays, there was not one which, read indulgently forty years afterwards, I found worthy of a place among my works ? "

We are fond of speaking of "a place in the world." In architecture that phrase finds its parallel in *site*. If you are given to the study of fine buildings, study how they are placed ; if the position be commanding and lend to the beauty of the edifice itself, or if it be ill-chosen and steal from it. When a great building like the Cathedral at Lincoln is well-placed, it is an everlasting pleasure to mankind. Crowning the hill-top, asserting itself with a power that at once wins and conquers, we feel how wise it was not to have placed that noble pile in the lower town. Even if Bishop Remigius' claim upon the high land drove the people into the fens it was for the best, for besides a magnificent building that shall stand royally for centuries, the lowland was drained, and you know how fair it is now, if you have ever seen it. So, building high in art has the same effect on the observer. We look back upon a life like that of Beethoven just as we do upon the great edifice I have mentioned ; it crowned a height because the conception of the builder placed it there. It is easier to build lower, and that is why so many do it. It is a curious fascination—that of winning renown or trying to win renown ; it is asking to-day to pay the tribute we do not deserve until a long time shall have tested the labor. How we run and stumble and get out of breath chasing about to catch a little glory, weaving our own wreath out of any leaf instead of waiting a while for the laurel tribute to be bestowed. The better the stones are shaped in the quarry the less noise of mallet and chisel there will be in the building. A place for every stone and no waste of space in ornament that has not some use; this is a good rule in any kind of building.

Art in a nation is much the same as stones in an edifice; the whole is excellent in proportion with the excellence of its parts. Every one of us who cares so much about art progress in America as to help it onward are units in the great whole—hence every one's work is the shaping of a single block; the better the quarrying is done the finer will the work be and the longer will it last. But the fault we often make is to think ourselves not single stones but buildings.

There are two other facts about the cathedrals which I like so much, that I will tell you, then I will end this talk, which means nothing whatever unless you find its parallel. Gothic architecture of the early Norman period has two distinctive features, wide-jointed masonry, and capitals left plain. This early Norman masonry " is extremely rude and bad; the joints between the stones are often from one inch to two or three inches wide, and filled with mortar not always of very good quality. In consequence of this imperfect construction, many of the towers fell down within a few years after their erection."* " Early in the twelfth century occurred the fall of the tower of Winchester Cathedral, celebrated from the peculiar circumstances with which it was accompanied, which are thus described by William of Malmesbury, who was living at that time. 'A few countrymen conveyed the body [of the king, William Rufus], placed on a cart, to the cathedral of Winchester, the blood dripping from it all the way. Here it was committed to the ground *within the tower*, attended by many of the nobility, but lamented by few. The next year the tower fell; though I forbear to mention the different opinions on this subject, lest I should seem to assent too readily to unsupported trifles, more especially that the building might have fallen *through imperfect construction*, even though he had never been buried there.'"†

I have already said that the people whose work lasts have built in hard material. The soft stone is easy to work, but the granites and porphyrys last. When layers of hard stone are brought closely together by the skill of the builder, his work bespeaks its own endurance. So it is told of Roger, Bishop

---

* "A B C of Gothic Architecture," John Henry Parker, p. 14.
† "Introduction to the Study of Gothic Architecture." J. H. Parker, pp. 47-48.

of Salisbury: he was "a prelate of great mind, and spared no expense toward completing his designs, especially in buildings. . . . . . He erected extensive edifices at vast cost and with surpassing beauty, *the courses of stone being so correctly laid that the joint deceives the eye and leads it to imagine that the whole wall is composed of a single block.*"

[The builder labors daily; and daily labor alone amounts to something. You are not, for your part, to expect Art or Literature to bring you deserved fame or chance success if you devote to it only an hour now and then, and that in a perfunctory manner. Not even a trade is learned in that way; so you may expect nothing to come from it in art, which demands such exquisite training of the mind and body. Dabblers in art and literature make a fatal error by setting any hope on what they do. To dash off a bit of rhyme to-day and another bit to-morrow, more for the sake of a pleasant moment than from a desire to say something, does not add anything to literature; it simply passes time for an idle man. It requires hard work to erect a building, symphony or cathedral, poem or monument. The stone of the brain, which is thought, must, like the thought of the earth, which is stone, be quarried and chipped, cut and carved, polished and placed, before it has any value. You who are earnestly devoting yourselves to the art-life are building; hence a hint to you, to learn some thing about it, should not be amiss.]

CHAPTER XXXIII.

WHAT IS SUCCESS IN ART?

Fame usually comes to those who are thinking about something else—very rarely to those who say to themselves; "Go to, now, let us be a celebrated individual."

Dr. O. W. Holmes.

It is strange what sensations of sublimity may spring from a very humble source.

This is the last of our talks. It has been, at least to me, the keenest delight to consider in the informal way we have adopted a few of the phases of art-life; more especially as they may influence us as musicians. It would be a great disappointment to me if, after all we have said about music and music-life, you could not write this chapter at least as well as I can. If, in sincerity, you have listened to what I have been pleased to say, you cannot fail to know that every artist, young or old, famed or obscure, has only two main reasons for devoting his time to art-work, they are, first, to find in such labor his best means for self-development and for becoming a useful being in the world; secondly, to recognize in art an admirable channel through which he may develop to the utmost powers given him by his Creator and assist others to do the same.   In plainer phrase, if art is ever a thing extraneous to him who calls himself its follower, he never once knows what it is to be an artist.   No success that is worth the having is a result of selfish motive.   Success means so much and yet so very little in these busy days of ours that I trust you understand me to mean by it only that which has resulted in making you a better man or woman, by no means what may have made you known afar, or made you wealthy, for these results are frequently the most pronounced symptoms of failure." Having passed a mountain chain one looks back upon it and sees its undulating outline to far better advantage than when he made his way along it. Far back in the first of these sixty or more talks we asked of one another in a very simple but earnest way, what was the motive of the music-life upon which we were entering. I would have you, now, look back upon the time when you entered the art-life you are now living and tell me truthfully how the mountain chain of events looks now; and remember, if you can what you felt and thought as you were passing through them.   Then let me ask you what you see in the perspective of the life behind you that has in a direct and forcible way tended to make you a more worthy child of the Creator—what you have done for others, in short, how your powers of thought and action have been used; whether for yourself in gain that can avail you nothing, or for yourself and others in a way that will make the world richer for your being. Such perspective glances at your art-life are very healthy indeed; indulge in them now and then, and be honest with yourself in the matter of what you see.

You will think of Fame and Gain. The first you will never get by seeking; a very little experience will prove this to you; gain is necessary in life, but it is not life, nor any considerable part of it. Commerce steps into art and sets its value upon this and that in its own clumsy way. When as an artist you must become at the same time a factor in the commerce of it, why may you not keep it in mind that there are other and more important influences guiding men than the gold-gain? Why should you, in earning what you need, wholly desert your duty and spend your time in storing up what you do not need? Always keep before you what is sufficient and what enough. To gain the one is a duty, the other may be your ruin. Always keep it before you that an active seeking after success ends either in popularity or failure. In the serious affairs of life you cannot afford to waste your one chance or any part of it in useless activity. Whatever you work in, makes you; for what you do and what you are, being the same, you cannot put the one behind the other. Every stone laid makes the building; but it is only honest service in the laying of them that makes it a great building. Not until you have learned to accept your work done as the reward for having done it will you have tasted of true success. " Honest service in art is rewarded by art " * You must first learn the satisfaction of that kind of reward, then never give a thought to success. Money cannot figure in art-life with more power than it figures in the purest love and friendship, and its power there is absolutely nothing.

You love art, to you it is lofty and idealistic, fairer than other things; you think the life in art must be more beautiful than the life in many humbler occupations practiced about us. Do not let that conception of your office so possess you that other thoughts more full of meaning do not follow. We are not to turn for results to what we do but to how we have done it; never mind what misconception of your worth and power your friends may make; if in their unthinking and enthusiastic way they credit you with what is not your due, their error, even if repeated by a nation of friends, does not really make you the possessor of what they would bestow upon you. [In assigning value to yourself as an active unit

---

* Wilkie Collins.

in the music world it is only what is in you that counts, not what you or your mistaken friends may think there is in you. This very plain statement of fact is lost to sight so frequently that by the judgment of others men lose sight of themselves. / Success is not boisterous, noisy and glittering. The flower-bud comes forth, enlarges in the sun, and the blossom comes soon, a type of loveliness, but the bursting of the bud is not accompanied by thunder; it comes forth as modestly, as noiselessly as the evening star, in the glowing western sky. The flower is born to bloom, the star to shine, and the greatest conceivable success lies in the doing of it.

What are the chief forces in the truest success an artist may have ? They are these :—

A well defined line of activity with a worthy motive at the far end of it.

Special ability, by birth and training, for developing fully that one line of activity.

A ready sympathy with all that is good in life.

A reverence for great ability in others.

A ready helping hand and a cheering word to the owners of one talent.

A consciousness that art is but one outlet for life; but one way of living it.

Lastly, that worth as an artist means not the noise you make but the good you do.

22

"One's reputation creeps along with tiny steps, like a dwarf, and must not be forced." *   When you see the second-hand of your watch making its way, with almost plainful slowness, over the space of a single minute, you think, perhaps, that the hours are passing by, but, really, it is life that is thus lessening bit by bit. So in art, the smallest actions mean the most.   The brook splashes noisily, while the sea moans.   The dabbler is heard, only the earnest worker is quiet.   The real workers must be looked for quite as often in unassuming places as elsewhere ; having a genuine and deep founded interest in what they do they step aside from the headlong strife and till the land that others race over.   They know how much better it is to be something, know something, work constantly and let success alone.   In any age only a few are to be known ; you may be of them, but do not let the possibility trouble you.   That these few may live many must labor to put the world in tune for them. This is where you all may find a place.   With no thought as to being known or unknown in future days do the most with what lies about you.   Your duty of the moment is the work in your hands. Dismiss it always with the feeling that it is well done.   Your statue is to be finished, not only in front but all around.

* Robert Schumann.

When you have taken the first step in your art career the work begins to end. One chip from the block of marble and the statue begins to come forth. What shall you think of as you work? of your chisel and mallet? or of what you are engaging them in? Think of what lies in the marble; there is a soul in it. The more magnificent the statue is to be, the greater must be your watchfulness. The greater the work you purpose to do, so greater the duty that rests upon you. We may not do as we please with the talent bestowed upon us. It is simply in our keeping. If you will study closely people about you, as well those out of the world of art as in it, you will find that men differ not only in the variety of their attainments *but in the intensity of them.* Now, it is the intensity of life that yields the success I would have you win. And such success is not let down upon you, one fine day, like a crown, but is always present in everything you do—and when all of you is not in what you are supposed to do then *you* are not doing it.

Not long life so much as deep life should be your hope. When the edifice is ill founded, its great height is its own misfortune. The oak is sturdy, because there is as much oak in the ground as above it. That is one of the countless lessons nature is constantly thrusting upon us, but they are so plain we do not see them. Still, why should we not welcome any old truth, if by obeying it we become a little more than we appear? The world is not wanting in wisdom, but in wisdom applied.

You must be ready to perceive quickly the wisdom of doing and not doing: " No man can produce great things who is not thoroughly sincere in dealing with himself, who would not exchange the finest show for the poorest reality, who does not so love his work that he is not only glad to give himself for it, but finds rather a gain than a sacrifice in the surrender."

I have said much by way of encouraging you to turn your thoughts into other channels than music. That is because I believe in the rewards of a gleaner. Like the fruits of earthly growth, so fruits of the mind come forth in variations of one manner. The history and meaning of art is so concealed in all arts that I cannot conceive a student of one of them to have no healthy curiosity regarding the others. Just as a mosaic is all the stones that form it, so art is the whole group and not one of them. Then, as I have always and shall always conceive you to be just a little more than you seem, I have always regarded you as artists by birth and training before I have thought of you as musicians. Regarding you as builders I see you recording yourselves not in soft stone but in hard—basalt and diorite. They last.   I do not think of you buried deep in art, but happy because art and life are one with you; then you are ready to find joy in its teachings and happiness in everything.   I would have you in ready, responding sympathy with every labor of your own and of others.   You should see with pleasure "the plucking of the grapes and all the labors of the field; the gathering of the flax and the harvesting of the wheat."   We strive to see poetry in these words when we are told that they come—as these do—from the Egyptian tomb of *Pi*, at Memphis, but why do we not ask ourselves why we do not see the poetry of the rural life we are living?   We are too prone to fancy that we see the reality in the reflection.

With the Greeks it was a law that gifts once consecrated to the gods could never again be used for profane purposes.   That reads like a law of nature, especially when we regard the cold statement as it concerns a nation of antiquity; but what have we to say of talents, that are gifts from God, which we consecrate in the morning of the art-life and desecrate before we are half-way on towards noon?   Is not that which we are so eager to do worth doing well?   If not, why should we worship it?

In the hands of such as you rests the art of this generation; you have received it and it will go from you.   It has come to you so great, and wonderful,

and fair that you are astonished at the richness of
your inheritance ; but think one point beyond your
transport—it must pass from you greater, more
wonderful, fairer than it is now. For the sake of
this duty do not lose yourself. One thoughtless
cut of the chisel and the statue in the block of
marble is a ruin ; yet you must be diligent or the
work will not be finished. "Work, Perses, that
hunger remain far from thee, and the beautifully-
wreathed Demeter be friendly to thee ; for the diligent are loved by the immortals."*

---

* Hesiod,

NOTE.

BOOKS REFERRED TO IN CHAPTER XVII.

ADLINE, ——, "A Dictionary of Art."

BAUDE, CHARLES ET ELIE PÉCAUT, "Simples Entretiens sur l'Art."

FERGUSSON, JAMES, "A History of Architecture."
"Illustrated Handbook of Architecture."

GOODYEAR, W. H., "A History of Art."

HUISH, M. B., "Japan and Its Art."

HUMPHREYS, HENRY NOEL, "The Illuminated Books of the Middle Ages." Illustrated by Owen Jones.

JONES, OWEN, "A Grammar of Ornament."
"Examples of Chinese Ornament."
"One Thousand and One Initial Letters."

LÜBKE, DR. WILHELM, "A History of Art." 2 Vols.

MITCHELL, LUCY M., "A History of Ancient Sculpture."
"Photographic Selections from Ancient Sculpture."

PAGE, I., "Guide for Drawing the Acanthus and Every Description of Ornamental Foliage."

PARKER, J. H., "A B C of Gothic Architecture."
"Introduction to the Study of Gothic Architecture."
"A Glossary of Terms Used in Grecian, Roman, Italian, and Gothic Architecture."

WHEATLEY, RICHARD, "Cathedral Architecture."

INDEX.*

---

* Formulated by Mr. Charles J. Roe.